ASPECTS OF SPIRIT
hun po, jing shen, yi zhi

MONKEY PRESS

Monkey Press is named after the Monkey King in The Journey to the West, the 16th century novel by Wu Chengen. Monkey blends skill, initiative and wisdom with the spirit of freedom, irreverence and a touch of mischief.

CHINESE MEDICINE FROM THE CLASSICS

Also in this series:

The Secret Treatise of the Spiritual Orchid: Suwen chapter 8
The Way of Heaven: Suwen chapters 1 and 2
The Heart in Lingshu chapter 8
The Lung
The Kidneys
The Liver
Spleen and Stomach
Heart Master, Triple Heater
Essence, Spirit, Blood and Qi
The Seven Emotions
The Eight Extraordinary Meridians
The Extraordinary Fu
A Study of Qi
Yin Yang in Classical Texts
The Essential Woman
Pregnancy and Gestation
Wu Xing: The Five Elements
Jing Shen: Huainanzi chapter 7
The Rhythm at the Heart of the World: Suwen chapter 5
The Double Aspect of the Heart

CHINESE MEDICINE FROM THE CLASSICS
Elisabeth Rochat de la Vallée

ASPECTS OF SPIRIT
hun po jing shen yi zhi
魂 魄 精 神 意 志

A Monkey Press Publication

Published by
Monkey Press
www.monkeypress.net
info@monkeypress.net

CHINESE MEDICINE FROM THE CLASSICS:
ASPECTS OF SPIRIT
hun po jing shen yi zhi
Elisabeth Rochat de la Vallée

© Monkey Press 2013

All rights reserved. No part of this book may be reproduced in any form without written permission from the publisher.

ISBN 978 1 872468 16 7

Transcribed and edited from a series of seminars organized by Orientation

Edited by Sandra Hill
Calligraphy: Qu Lei Lei
Printed and bound in the UK by Short Run Press

CONTENTS

Foreword	viii
HUN AND PO (heavenly and earthly souls)	1
The characters for hun and po	4
HUN AND PO IN THE EARLIEST TEXTS	7
The hun and dreams	11
Differentiation of hun and po	13
The hun and po at death	16
Chunqiu Zuozhuan	18
Rituals at death	25
The Book of Rites: Liji	27
Baihutong	29
SUMMARY	30
The number of the hun and po	31
HUN AND PO IN MEDICAL TEXTS	34
Lingshu chapter 8	34
Pathology in Lingshu chapter 8	44
HUN AND PO IN OTHER MEDICAL TEXTS	46
Lingshu chapter 80	48
Lingshu chapter 9	50
Lingshu chapter 47	51
Lingshu chapter 54	53

JING SHEN (vital spirit)	59
Spirits and wind	60
The character shen	62
The character jing	63
JING SHEN IN CLASSICAL TEXTS	64
Chunqiu Zuozhuan	66
Duke Zhuang, year 32	66
Duke Zhuang, year 6	68
Duke Zhuang, year 10	69
Lunyu: Analects of Confucius	71
Xunxi: Change and transformation	73
Huainanzi	77
Xici	78
Zhuangzi	78
The Historical Records of Sima Qian	82
Guanzi: chapter 49 Neiye	86
Huainanzi chapter 1	87
Huainanzi chapter 7	88
Huainanzi chapter 2	90
Spirits and Qi	90
JING ESSENCES	94
Guanzi: chapter 49 Neiye	94
Huainanzi chapter 7	98
Xunzi chapter 21	99
Lüshi chunqiu chapter 3 section II	99
JING SHEN	100
SHEN AND JING SHEN IN MEDICAL TEXTS	103
Suwen chapter 5	103
Suwen chapter 1	104
Suwen chapter 71	105
Spirits and the Heart	106

YI ZHI (intent and will)	121
The character yi	121
YI IN CLASSICAL TEXTS	124
Daxue, The Great Learning	126
Guanzi: Neiye	130
Chunqiu fanlu	130
Guanzi: Neiye	132
ZHI IN CLASSICAL TEXTS	135
The character zhi	135
Lunyu, Analects of Confucius	137
Mencius IIA	140
Duke Zhao 25th year	141
Lüshi Chunqiu chapter 4	145
YI IN MEDICAL TEXTS	146
Suwen chapter 44	147
Suwen chapter 25	149
Suwen chapter 54	150
Lingshu chapter 8	151
ZHI IN MEDICAL TEXTS	157
Suwen chapter 2	161
Suwen chapter 39	163
YI AND ZHI AS A COUPLE	167
INDEX	170
BIBLIOGRAPHY	177

FOREWORD

Defining 'spirit', whether in a western or eastern context, is bound to be fraught with difficulties. And in attempting to determine what the Chinese literati of the 2nd century BCE meant by the spirits in the context of the Chinese medical literature, we must form our understanding by looking at the ideas and beliefs current at that time. This is the aim of this book.

It is important to be aware of differences – both in culture and in historical time – but we must also not forget that we are human beings, and as such share with the ancient Chinese the experience of what it means to be human. We share the same bodily structure and the same possibility for consciousness, and can therefore appreciate the ways in which different cultures have reached an understanding of consciousness, its relationship with the physical body and with the cosmos.

So in order to understand the notion of spirit within the classical medical texts, and particularly those of the Huangdi Neijing (The Yellow Emperor's Inner Classic), we need to look at the classical texts of Confucianism, Daoism and other schools of thought which formed the context for the thinking of the time. The medical texts have a particular interest in the relationship between body and spirit; the notion of the *wu shen* (五 神), or five aspects of spirit, is quite specific to the medical literature, and is part of the development of five phase (*wu xing* 五 行) theory at the time. This theory of correspondence posits *shen* (神) as related to the heart and fire, *hun* (魂) to the liver and wood, *po* (魄) to the lung and metal, *yi* (意, generally translated as intent) to the spleen and earth, and *zhi* (志, will), or in some contexts *jing* (精, vital essences) to the kidneys.

But within the context of this separation into five, it must always be understood that there is a unity, a oneness, which defines the individual self and which may be described as spirit, soul, awareness, consciousness, mind – as well as emotion, feeling and sensitivity. The five element framework is a tool that may be used to analyse these various aspects of the whole. Consequently, in each expression of spirit there is always something which pertains to the whole – all the faculties combine to form a 'self'.

Feelings and emotions may be contained within the idea of *shen* (神) and in the same way, both *yi* and *zhi* may contain something quite spiritual. The English words 'intent' and 'will' are not enough to translate the complexity of these terms. *Yi* and *zhi* allude to all that is perceived, learned and understood; everything that forms the way in which the mind functions, with all its individual inclinations and propensities. They are therefore responsible for the disposition of the heart/mind, and help the formation of the individual inner reality – the spirit and the soul.

So we can see that there are three particular problems that may arise when approaching this subject. Firstly, within the medical texts, each of the characters of the five aspects of spirit is used both in the five phase context mentioned above, and in the more general context of the philosophical literature of the time. It is therefore vital to understand each reference in relation to its specific context.

Secondly, the English words used in translation can never reflect the exact meaning of the Chinese characters. If we take the character *shen* (神), for example, possible translations into English may be: spirit, spirits, soul, gods, deities, spiritual beings, immortals, supernatural, wondrous, miraculous, mysterious, mystical, appearance, looks, mind, expressions, smart, clever… A word or character may be used at many different levels and we understand the meaning within an accepted cultural context. At the same time, several Chinese characters may be translated as spirit or soul given the appropriate context. In English, we similarly use the words spirit and soul with quite different and specific meanings. Not to be aware of the context leads to misapprehension, misinterpretation and misconception.

Thirdly, the ideas presented here are not easy to comprehend, whether in Chinese or English, but *shen* is not a pure abstraction – it is an attempt to name something that human beings have perceived and experienced. The same is true of *hun* and *po*. And we can begin to understand these ideas by referring to our own experience of what we may define as soul or spirit. How might we define these terms today? Does spirit include something mental or intellectual that is perhaps not a part of the definition of soul? Is soul more the sensitive, emotional aspect? Meanings are complex and intricate.

So we are not attempting here to make a decisive definition of soul or spirit, but it is possible to say one or two things that are specific to the Chinese understanding – and particularly to their understanding of spirit and soul in relationship with the body.

The relationship between body, mind and spirit is an intermingling – but one in which each aspect retains its own status, function and place in the hierarchy of life. If the body is deprived of sustenance, the mind will not function well. When one is unable to eat well enough to nourish the body, the mind weakens, thinking is more difficult, the memory vacillates and the will wavers. Human behaviour is then driven more by hunger than by the reasoning of the heart/mind. But if one can cultivate the vital spirit (*jing shen* 精 神) to a sufficient quality, one is able to act with integrity and humanity even when hungry, and share with others, rather than kill for food.

The spirit is closely linked to the very quality of the substance of the body, to the physical heart and to the blood, but it is also free from them and capable of independent action. In our present physical life, the spirit needs physical reality in order to express itself. And that physical reality needs to be controlled and inspired by the spirit.

Elisabeth Rochat de la Vallée

Paris, 2013

This book has been adapted and edited from three separate seminars given in London over a period of two years. We have decided to keep the original pattern of the lectures, and the sections reflect their chronology, beginning with the *hun* and *po*, moving on to *jing shen*, and concluding with *yi* and *zhi*. Each section examines the characters for each term, followed by examples of their usage in the classical philosophical texts, and concludes with a selection from the medical texts of the Huangdi Neijing, Suwen and Lingshu. Translations from the Chinese are by Elisabeth except where indicated. As with all the Monkey Press books, our aim is to bring clarity, but not at the expense of authenticity. The English translation always aims to reflect the classical Chinese meaning rather than comply with modern medical terminology.

Because of her intimate knowledge of both the medical and philosophical texts of this period, Elisabeth is uniquely placed within the scholarship of classical Chinese medicine. We are very fortunate that she has brought the depth of her understanding and insight to this fascinating and often misunderstood subject.

Sandra Hill

London, 2013

Diagrammatic representation of the Mawangdui funeral banner

The cover image is adapted from a detail of the Mawangdui funeral banner, and shows the seven *po* (or earthly souls) receiving nourishment before they are guided to the underworld.

The banner was excavated in 1972 from one of three barrows (one of which had been vandalized) on the outskirts of Changsha, the capital of the ancient kingdom of Chu, and present capital of Hunan Province. An inscription in the main tomb dates the burial to 163 BCE, and identifies the tomb as that of the Marquis of Dai. The banner was discovered in a second tomb which contained the body of a woman, considered to be the wife of the Marquis. A triple layered coffin had been used, which ensured the extraordinary preservation of the body as well as of the painting, which was draped over the inner coffin.

Made as a talisman and guide to the souls of the departed, the banner throws an interesting light on the views of life and death at the end of the third, and the beginning of the second century BCE. In the diagram opposite, it is possible to make out two dragons in the lower, narrower, part of the banner, which cross at the centre and represent the intertwining of *yin* and *yang* to create the flow of life; below the knot that is formed by their union, the seven *po*, or earthly souls of the woman can be seen receiving food and drink before they make their descent into the underworld – the lowest part of the banner peopled by sea creatures and demons. Directly above the knot of life, the three *hun*, or heavenly souls, wait behind the figure of the Marchioness to be guided to the spirit worlds above.

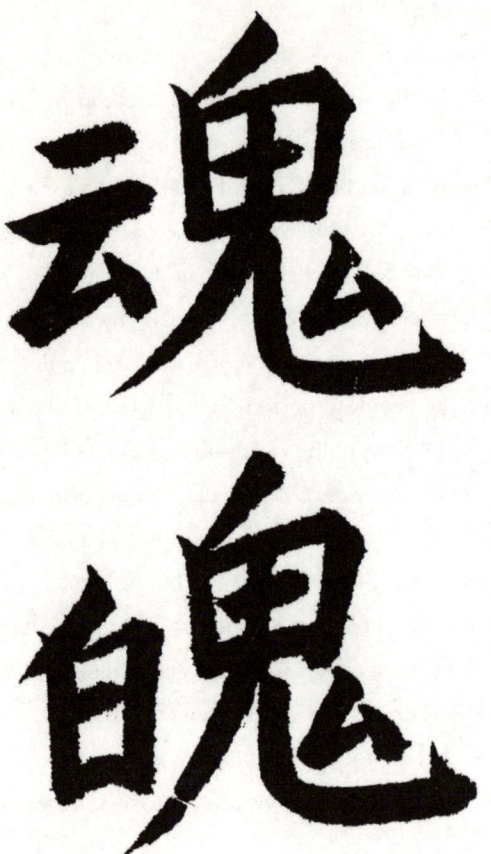

hun po

HUN AND PO

The concept of *hun* (魂) and *po* (魄) is part of a very ancient system of ideas and beliefs in China, and both terms appear in the earliest texts. *Hun* and *po* are often translated into western languages as 'souls', in the plural, because there are both *hun* and *po* souls, and possibly several of each. In our attempt to understand these terms, this becomes problematic, because who really knows what the soul is? Of course we can find a definition of soul in the dictionary, and we all may speak of our soul, but it is very difficult to give a clear definition of what we mean. Even within Christian theology, there is no definition of the soul. On the other hand, I do not know of any human civilization which does not speak of something which we would translate or understand as the soul.

If we concentrate on China, or Southeast Asia, there is certainly an idea of something which is not the body, but which is a part of each individual life, able to exist independently from the body. This is not only found within the shamanic tradition; in most cultures there is the idea that souls are able to travel, and that in doing so it is important for them not to get lost. In the geographical area of China and Southeast Asia, anthropologists from the 19th and 20th centuries have discovered evidence of this kind of belief system in very remote and primitive villages, where there has been little evolution of civilization. It was certainly the common belief some thousands of years ago that souls were able to travel, both while alive and after death, and a similar kind of belief system has remained in some of the more remote communities. We find the same thing in Europe – in various books written by scholars and theologians of the middle ages and even later – but there is also evidence in the practices of the common people. Certainly at the very moment of death, even unbelieving scholars may have a different perspective! No-one knows for sure, and there will always be several levels of understanding in each country and each civilization.

When you read stories about ghosts and phantoms or tales of the benevolent or malevolent spirits of the dead returning, there are always several levels of understanding possible within those ideas. There are also many different literary styles, and many different approaches, including the idea of the evolution of the soul, which is found in early Daoism. The arrival of Buddhism in China introduced the idea of the development of the soul's sensitivity – and this led to the various uses of the terms *hun* and *po* in Buddhism which consequently affected the Daoism of the 9th 10th and 11th centuries CE.

So this is a complex subject. But here I will concentrate on material from the early texts dating from before and around the beginning of the common era, and I will base my presentation only on texts – which is to say that I will not speak of other aspects of beliefs – tales, legends, ghosts and so on, even though one or two texts may allude to those ideas.

We know that from the very beginning of written records in China the belief existed that human beings have a soul which leaves at death; what we call 'ancestor worship' is based on this. This is not exactly a faith, but more a vision of life and human destiny. It is difficult for our human consciousness to imagine that we will disappear entirely. We also believe that if we are able to see, to hear, to think – that there must also be something more than the body. We might all have the same eyes, but we see things differently. We feel that we see differently – but what is this self that is feeling if it is not my eyes and my body and my bones? It is all of those things, but it is also something more, something that allows understanding, perception, consciousness, awareness and so on – and maybe that is not part of the body. So if it is not part of the body, maybe it becomes free of the body after death, and maybe it will even remain powerful after the body has gone. It was therefore important to take care of the ancestors after death, and the *hun* came to be understood as the spirits of the dead that ascended to heaven.

But we will see that there is a difference between the notion of the soul in the East and in the West. In the West, this vision of the body and soul leads – especially at the end of the middle ages and the renaissance, 15th-16th centuries CE – to the division and separation between the body and the soul. The body is physical and will decompose and disappear, whereas the soul is seen as an immortal principle linked to God, and judged by God. In the West the soul is often understood in opposition to the body, and this is a very important difference between the Chinese and western perspectives.

Both have the same basic idea of the soul, which is different, and in a way separate from the body, and which can leave the body, not only at death, but in dreams and at certain stages of meditation. But from the Chinese perspective, it is not possible to say that there is a separation between the soul and the body. This is because the *po* are also souls and they are definitely linked to the body, even incorporated into the body, and as we will see, in some texts they are almost synonymous with the body. So on the one hand, there are similarities between the eastern and western concepts, but on the other hand there are differences.

Another problem that we encounter when looking at these texts is that the meaning and the use of *hun* and *po* is not consistent. Each of the characters in Chinese may have various meanings depending on the date and also the kind of text. The common meaning of *hun* and *po* is found in the medical texts, but, as in other branches of knowledge, there may also be very specific uses of these terms which are not the same as the common use, for example in ritual. I will try to clarify the meaning of these concepts in each different context.

The characters for hun and po

We will start with the characters for *hun* (魂) and *po* (魄). The part common to both is the character *gui* (鬼) which means the spirits of earth, as opposed to the *shen* (神) the spirits of heaven. As we will see, this character *gui* (鬼) refers to all the forces and powers of the earth, but it may also be used for ghosts, spirits which have an attachment to the earth. As the character *gui* forms part of both the *hun* and *po*, it suggests that both are related to a life which takes form and develops on earth. As we will see, the *hun* are often described as relating more to heaven, the *po* to earth, but it is not possible to analyse a character and its etymology or origin using meaning that the character will take on later. The character *hun* was not as closely related to heaven in the early texts as it came to be during the 3rd and 2nd centuries BCE.

Ancestral worship aimed to call the souls of the deceased back to the place of the ritual; to return from their current abodes – whether above or below. In this context, the character *gui* (鬼) has a relationship with another character *gui* (歸) which means to return, and it is possible that both characters *hun* and *po* have a relationship with the idea of a return – possibly the temporary return facilitated by the ritual, or the return of ghosts coming to haunt both the people and places associated with their past life and death.

The character *gui* (鬼) goes back to the oracular inscriptions (*jia gua wen* 甲骨文, 14th - 13th centuries BCE) where it is often used with the general meaning of the souls of the dead. Later the character was associated with *shen*, the spirits of heaven, forming the expression *gui shen*, which represents all the powers acting on earth and in heaven, and their intermingling between. In later texts, the souls of the deceased are also distinguished as *hun* and *po*.

Life is always expressed as a double movement reflecting heaven and earth; this is characteristic of all life, but especially that of the human being, who exists between heaven and earth. The *hun* and *po* are therefore different from the spirits (*shen* 神), which are definitely from heaven and represent the natural order of life. But there is a strong relationship between the *hun* and the *shen*, because the fulfilment of the *hun* within an individual is to become *shen*-like. Spirits of the ancestors (*hun* 魂) ascend to heaven and become *shen* (神), spirits of heaven.

We have to remember that *hun*, *po* and *shen* are not always used together or in relation one with the other. According to the context, each may take on a specific meaning or even double the meaning of the other.

The phonetic part of the character *hun* (魂) conveys the idea of clouds (*yun* 云), ascending by evaporation and accumulating on high. Several texts written at the beginning of the common era used phonetic and graphic correlations to express the nature of the *hun*. The clouds moving constantly in the sky give the image of the *hun* journeying, travelling constantly with no limitations. The journey of the soul is the journey of the *hun*; but the *hun*, being linked to the *yang*, are also characterized by movement and activity and are therefore also likened to the *qi*. Free and easy movement characterizes the *hun*; they are able to escape from the body and wander in the realm of the spirits – temporarily, or for eternity.

The phonetic part of *po* (魄) is the colour white (*bai* 白), possibly relating to the colour of the bones, which remain when the body has decayed back into the earth. After some years the bones become white and remain as the skeleton when everything else has disappeared. In later five element cosmology, white became the colour related to metal, to the west and to the lung; a colour linked with the descending movement and the return to the earth. These associations were not yet made in the earliest use of this character, but thanks to its relationship with the bones, the white colour was already linked with the return to earth of the bodily remains, and also with the aging process. As we grow old the colour of the hair has the tendency to turn white – which is of course more visible in a society where there is only black hair. This is also seen in nature, where the arrival of white frosts and snow signifies the winter, with its action of burying within. So white is an indication of the gradual decline and return of the body to the earth.

We see in several texts that the character *hun* (魂) is linked with the *yang*, with movement and with a quickening; there is a tendency to move quickly, possibly too quickly. It is the *yang* ability that is often characterized by a fiery race horse, which is also used as an image of the *hun*. The Shuowen Jiezi (a book published in 121 CE on the etymology and meaning of characters, which forms the basis of Wieger's 'Chinese Characters') says that the *hun* are the *yang qi*. At that time the theory of *yin* and *yang* was well defined, which was not the case five or six centuries earlier. Throughout all this time there is a development of the concept of the *hun*, and this analogy with the *yang qi* suggests that if the *hun* are no longer in the body, the body is inert and without movement, like a corpse. But the character *hun* (魂) is also used for the mind, and specifically for the ability to know and to be aware – the individual consciousness. It is also related to the ability to understand and perceive, to relate things, to think and to feel; it is more related to movement than to substance, closer to what has no form (*wu xing* 無形), like the spirits, *shen* (神).

By its ability to move and to penetrate, *hun* has the meaning of individual awareness — it is the ability of each individual to perceive and to understand. It suggests the individual self, that which moves each one of us. If my soul is moved, I am moved. That is quite a common use of *hun* found even in the early texts, where it may have the meaning of everything that is felt — all emotion, knowledge and ideas.

HUN AND PO IN THE EARLIEST TEXTS

Chu was the name of one of the states forming China before the unification of the empire in 221 BCE. This was an area of southern China where imagination was vivid and myths and legends flourished. There is a series of songs or poems, the post important written by several different authors during the 4th and 3rd centuries BCE, known as the Chuci, or Songs of Chu. In one of these songs, the poet's soul is tormented:

'In the night-time I lay wide-eyed without sleeping, my unquiet soul (*hun* 魂) active until the daylight.'

In other texts of the 3rd century BCE, for example the Lüshi Chunqiu (Spring and Autumn Annals of Lü Buwei), it is possible to see the character *hun* used in the same way — to be worried and concerned, over-tired and sad with anxiety, or carried away with an idea or with beauty — and for the *shen* (神) to be exhausted and the *hun* injured.

'Their delightful conception stirs one to the bone and marrow and their bewitching phrases captivate the soul (*hun* 魂).'

This is a very common use of *hun* in classical Chinese. At this time the character *hun* was also used for supernatural beings no longer belonging to the earth, the spirits of the ancestors, deities and so on. Very often it is linked with other characters, especially the character *ling* (靈). In modern Chinese *hun* is also used to speak of the soul of the country, and is very close to the way that we may use the word soul in the West.

If we turn to the general use and meaning of *po*, in the Shuowen Jiezi, the *po* are presented as the *yin* spirits (陰 神) attached to the earth, to form and to substance. There is very often the suggestion that the *po* are linked to the body, they cannot escape, whereas the *hun* fly away in dreams and meditation. At the very moment of death, the *hun* leave the body, so the body is motionless and without the ability to perceive or to feel. In some cases, *po* has almost the same meaning as the body itself, but the *po* are not the body as such, they are the powers of life which belong to the earth, to substance, but particularly to the body. They may be seen as the desire to live, which is not the same as the awareness of the *hun*. They are the life of the body which operates without the influence of thought and consciousness – breathing, digesting, circulating the blood, maintaining metabolism.

The *po* cannot separate from the body and the substance of the body, so they remain attached. They cannot travel or wander, but are held within the body, so when the body decomposes, they pass with the material substance of the body back to the earth. They may remain attached to the bones, and when the bones finally dry up, they become the power of the substance of the earth again.

Po is sometimes used for the manifestation of the life of the body which can be seen in the face and in the attitude. It can also be used for a certain kind of vitality and strength of the life force, which is different from the awareness and cleverness of the *hun*. It is possible to be very aware, but unable to act because the body does not have the strength. So it may be strength, not only of the physical body, but of courage which is an aspect of the life force.

Hun and *po* are used together with the meaning of an individual life, and we can find an example of that in Zhuangzi chapter 22. Speaking of life and death, the Zhuangzi makes a comparison between the fleeting nature of human life and the jump of a young colt over a ravine; the beginning of the jump is birth, and when the colt touches the earth again on the other side, it is death. There is a transformation, and there is a living being; there is another transformation, and the life is over. But what is life? It is simply this movement. The *hun* and *po* leave and the body accomplishes its return.

We can also see this in the Chunqiu Zuozhuan, 25th year:

'What gives subtle understanding to the heart is called *hun* and *po*. Once *hun* and *po* have departed how can a human being remain?'
心 之 精 爽 是 謂 魂 魄
xin zhi jing shuang shi wei hun po
魂 魄 去 之 何 以 能 久
hun po qu zhi he yi neng jiu

The distinction between *hun* and the *po* is not the main point here, they are taken together as the total and complete animation of the being. They are spoken of as a couple which indicate all life, and this represents the general understanding of *hun* and *po* in the 4th and 3rd centuries BCE, they are presented as a couple, which together make and maintain life according to the principles of heaven and earth. When they come together, there is life, and when they are no longer together, there is death – also called the final transformation. What is important is to nourish and maintain them, to cultivate them – and they have to be cultivated and maintained together.

We find this idea in many texts, for example in Huainanzi chapter 21, a text from the 2nd century BCE:

'Thus, human beings are able to cultivate and nourish their vital spirit (*jing shen* 精 神), quieten the *hun* and *po*. This is the way in which they are able to maintain their true nature, and strengthen and preserve the abode of emptiness and nothingness (*xu wu* 虛 無).'

In some texts there are instructions on the way to cultivate *hun* and *po* and to maintain them carefully, which is the same as to fully realize life and to prepare for integration into the *dao*. Human beings must take care of the *hun* and *po*, nourish, maintain and cultivate them in the correct way. They represent a kind of evolving reality, not something which is given and which does not change, but the power of heaven and the power of earth within each human being, which will evolve within each individual according to the way they live and the way they behave. The quality of *hun* and *po* is dependent on individual behaviour – we may realize their potential fully, partially or poorly, and this ability is something that we have from the foetal stage of gestation and pregnancy, which is the time when life is built. Within each human being there is this double potential, they are of the earth, but with the double power and potential of heaven and earth within human life.

The hun and dreams

In Huainanzi chapter 7, when speaking of a sage or an authentic human being, it is said that their sleep is without dreams. This is also found in Zhuangzi chapter 6, and it implies that there is no stimulation, no excitement, nothing is disturbed. If everything is at peace, what would the dream be about? Dreams are seen here as an agitation of the soul (as we also see in Neijing Lingshu chapter 43), a lack of harmony in the being. If everything is perfectly calm, why would we dream? On the other hand there may be dreams (and this is mentioned in Zhuangzi chapter 2) which are more of an authentic relationship with heaven, with the spirits of heaven or the ancestors. In this case there is no real difference between dreaming and contemplation or meditation. It is a kind of meeting or wandering of the souls.

When a text such as the Zhuangzi says that the authentic man does not dream, it means that there is nothing disturbing the balance and harmony of his life. Nothing is able to excite the movement that creates dreams during the night. When awake they do not worry, and as a result the *po* do not sink into the depths and the *hun* do not jump up, or bound away, like a startled horse. An authentic human being is able to nourish life, harmonizing *yin* and *yang qi* in such a way that the *po* do not simply sink, and the *hun* do not rear up. This means that they are not only able to remain together, but also that they are in a balanced relationship, and thus ensure life. Within both mind and body there is neither depression nor over-excitement – there is no imbalance at any level. The rising movement and the descending movement are in perfect balance, in the digestive tract as well as in thought.

It is important to remember that the *po* are not simply the body. They not only represent the substances of the body – the flesh, the bones, the body fluids – but also all the movements and transformations of these substances which are part of bodily life but which are not controlled by the will or the conscious mind. Throughout life, a human being has to remain attached to the earth while aspiring to heaven; that this can be achieved without one aspect harming the other is the prefect balance of the spiritual and corporeal – of body and mind.

Question: There is an interpretation of dreams in medicine. Is this simply an agitation of this kind?

Again, it depends on what kind of dream. Dreams can be pathological and in that case are an indication of imbalance. But we can have dreams which are not. In this case they are simply a meeting with what is heavenly – which could be a meeting with the ancestors, with nature, or simply with the reality of things as they are. It is also possible to have dreams, for example within a temple, which enable us to see things; this is a clarity of the mind. In Daoist texts, such as the Zhuangzi, dreams are considered more as a disturbance, as a kind of counterpart while asleep of the functioning of the intellect and desires while awake.

'The true man of ancient times slept without dreaming and woke without care.' (Zhuangzi chapter 6)

But for others, such as Confucius, dreams may be seen as a blessing. Confucius himself was said to long to see his famous and virtuous ancestor, the Duke of Zhou, in his dreams, in order to communicate with him and receive inspiration from his ancestor's spirit.

In medicine dreams may be an indication of an imbalance. If the imbalance is very severe, there may be a pathology of excessive dreaming, which is linked with the quality of the blood. Nightmares are often linked to the liver and the blood. The heart or the kidneys may also be involved, it depends on the particular circumstances. In treatment, it is also possible to unblock some restriction which will reveal itself in dreams, and then it will calm down. In dreams we may be able to see an imbalance which we cannot see when awake. The correct interpretation of this image is the skill!

> 'When *yin qi* is in excess, then one dreams of wading through water and one is fearful; when *yang qi* is in excess, one dreams of great fires and burning. When both *yin* and *yang qi* are in excess, then one dreams of killing and maiming. When the *qi* is in excess above, one dreams of flying; when the *qi* is in excess below, one dreams of falling.' (Suwen chapter 17)

Differentiation of hun and po

The texts such as the Huainanzi provide an early example of the way in which *hun* and *po* are used together; it is their coming together that produces life. But at the same time, and within the same texts, a differentiation may be made between *hun* and *po*. Speaking generally, we can simply say '*hun* and *po*' to mean souls, but they can also be differentiated according to their specific aspects, for example in Huainanzi chapter 9:

> 'The *qi* of heaven (*tian qi* 天氣) makes the *hun*,
> the *qi* of earth (*di qi* 地氣) makes the *po*.
> 天 氣 為 魂 地 氣 為 魄
> *tian qi wei hun, di qi wei po*

'Returning to their primal dwelling, each keeps their own abode.
反 之 玄 房 各 處 其 宅
fan zhi xuan fang, ge chu qi zhai

'The one who is able to preserve them and not lose them,
will commune (*tong* 通) above with the Great One (*tai yi* 太 一),
守 而 勿 失 上 通 太 一
shou er wu shi shang tong tai yi

'the vitality (essence, *jing* 精) of the Great One communes with the way of heaven (*tian dao* 天 道).'
太 一 之 精 通 於 天 道
tai yi zhi jing tong yu tian dao

The *hun* are made by the *qi* of heaven, the *po* by the *qi* of earth. If human beings are a meeting of the *qi* of heaven and earth, then each being has the *qi* of heaven and the *qi* of earth within them, and these are the foundation of human life. Within each new life there is an exchange and meeting of heaven *qi* and earth *qi*, and this can occur only through the union of male and female. But it is not simply the essences of a man and a woman that are able to give life; because they are living beings, they are able to transmit life to another being. Through them there is a meeting of what is able to give life, and that is a meeting of these opposite and complementary powers – the expression of the oneness that is heaven and earth.

Everything that exists in the universe is made in that way, there is always a double aspect to the power of life, and at a very basic level that is called *hun* and *po*. The power of heaven is developed as subtlety and cleverness, the *qi* without form, and the power of earth is more the activity and strength within substance.

Through the rising up and dispersing movement of the *yang*, the taking form and condensing movement of the *yin* is able to manifest. These double movements operate at the level of the whole person, the *hun* being associated with the movement of the mind, the emotions, the feelings and awareness, which are considered as heavenly. The ability to be aware and have consciousness is the manifestation of heaven within us. The *po* is the manifestation of earth, and is the strength and the life of the body, but it is also that which is able to sustain the *hun*.

So there is also this interdependency – we cannot live without either *hun* or *po*. But heaven always has some kind of precedence over earth. There is the same relationship between *hun* and *po* as between heaven and earth. Heaven initiates and orders and earth follows. Anyone who abandons the heavenly aspect would be going against this, developing only the earthly side, satisfying their appetites and desires on the physical level. There may be nothing wrong with that, but if it is not under the authority and command of heaven, which is also the awareness and cleverness that can be cultivated as the power of heaven within, then the body will suffer, and it may not be possible to accomplish human destiny.

These ideas are presented in the classical Chinese texts. There is a complete inter-dependency, but at the same time a hierarchy, as in the relationship between heaven and earth. There cannot be earth without heaven and even heaven without earth – it is not possible – but at the same time, the relationship is a hierarchical one, they are not equal in that way. The body has its needs and desires, but the mind must control them, because the body's needs are not self-regulating, and have a tendency to become excessive. One never has enough. It is through awareness and consciousness that we learn when to stop, when enough is enough.

The hun and po at death

We have seen that the *hun* and *po* make up an individual human life, but also that the *hun* and *po* themselves are a result of our lives and the way that we live. At death there is a separation, a partition, and the *hun* leave the body. The *po* do not have the same mobility, the same ability to move as the *hun*, so the *po* remain within the body and the *hun* rise. The *hun* are often said to rise and become the spirits of the ancestors, and in this context, *hun* is linked with the character *ling* (靈), which means benevolent influences, or spiritual influence. The spirits of the ancestors are often called *hun ling* (魂 靈). The *hun* having now achieved their heavenly nature.

In the archaic vision, the ancestors were much more powerful than the living, able to affect their offspring in a good or bad way – to send them blessings or curses. We know from oracular inscriptions that in ancient times, for example around 13th and 12th centuries BCE, there was an aspect of medicine which involved finding the offended ancestor who had sent disease to the village, family or individual, and repairing that relationship with ritual. But this is very much a part of shamanism, and even sorcery; it is not medicine as it is understood later.

There was a slow evolution of these ideas and relationships, and by the time of the 8th century BCE, it was still more or less powerful, and the people still believed in this kind of thing. After a few more centuries it would be more difficult to threaten people, or educated people at least, with an ancestral curse. But the idea of the survival of the soul after death remained, as did ancestral worship as the maintenance and nourishment of the spirits of the ancestors. It became a way of not only avoiding ancestral curses, but also a way of allowing the ancestors to keep their strength and power, and of continuing their existence. This was achieved by being pure in heart and thinking of them, by keeping their memory alive. But it could also be achieved with music and offerings; the smells emanating from offerings of fruits and meats being able to attract the souls of the departed. The souls would be nourished in this way, and it was thought possible to re-unite the *hun* and *po* for a while and to give them substance. This is the nature of filial piety – simply to take care of the souls of the ancestors, which need the support of the living in order to survive.

> 'The *hun* and *qi* (or the *hun*-like *qi*, *hun qi* 魂 氣) return (*gui* 歸) to heaven, while the body and *po* (or the *po* attached to the body-form, *xing po* 形 魄) return (*gui* 歸) to the earth. From this came the principle of carefully looking for them in the *yin* and *yang*.' (Liji, Book of Rites)

Here, the *yin* represent the realm of darkness, inside the depths of the earth where the body is buried in the 'yellow sources', the abode of the *po*. The *yang* represents the realm of light above, where clouds and *qi* circulate, in heaven – the abode of the *hun*. To search for the *po*, libations and heavy fragrances which penetrate the earth were used. To search for the *hun*, they used light fragrances which would ascend to the air and pass across the roof of the temple. In the case of the *hun*, the support is not in material form, it is in the smell, the fragrance, the sound of music and also the feeling in the heart of the descendants. For the *po* it is a bit different. In The Book of Rites there are several chapters devoted to the ceremonies made at the various stages of a funeral, and also to the rituals used for the deceased at various stages after burial. This text does not refer directly to the *po*, the vocabulary is not that fixed, but it is the same kind of thing:

'While the bones and flesh return to the earth (*tu* 土) it is their destiny, the *hun qi* (魂 氣) are able to travel and to spread everywhere.'

This again shows the difference between what rises and spreads and what slowly dissolves back into the earth. This same idea is found in other texts which relate more directly to the *hun* and *po*. When something goes wrong at death, it is usually that the *po* souls do not gradually dissolve into the earth, but remain somewhere with a kind of strength. This shows that the *po* is not simply the body, because the body is in the coffin, but there is a force, which resembles the body of the departed person, and which can harm the living – it is a kind of ghost. We notice here again that the *hun* are linked with the *qi*. The *qi* are formless, invisible, intangible as opposed to the body, the bones and the flesh.

Chunqiu Zuozhuan

There is something similar in the Chunqiu Zuozhuan, which is a commentary to the Chunqiu, the Spring and Autumn Annals. It is arranged according to the reign of the Dukes of the kingdom of Lü; each chapter having the name of the Duke and the year of his reign. This is Duke Zhao 7th year.

A man has been executed, and the problem is that he was not a criminal. This was not only unfair, but the man was of very high rank and from a powerful family, many family members being high ranking ministers in the kingdom. This indicates that there was a strength to his lineage. People within high ranking families were able to nourish themselves with the best that was available, so their vitality, their essences were good and strong. Because of the strength of their essences, they were able to nourish and sustain their life force, and even their skill and ability, so they made good ministers. This ability to maintain a good quality of life also gives strength to bones and the flesh, so the *po* are nourished. When a man of that calibre dies suddenly and unfairly, the strength of the *po* may remain and become a ghost. In this situation it is necessary to guide this strength back to where it belongs – to help it to return, but it needs a place to return to, a grave or a sepulchre. It is dangerous if someone is not buried. Rituals are important too, not only at the actual burial, but it is important to carry out the appropriate rituals at the appropriate times, and to provide something for the soul to eat.

'When the *gui* (鬼) have a place to return to, they will not become malicious.'

Gui (鬼) in this context is the same as the *po* – or perhaps relates to both the *hun* and *po* inappropriately coming back amongst the living. But the usual belief will be that at death the *hun* become *shen* and the *po* become *gui*. The character used for to return to is *gui* (歸) – it is common to use characters with the same pronunciation in these texts. The strength of the *po* does not know where to go, or how to return to the place that it belongs to, which is the earth. If the *po* cannot return, they come back to the world of the living and become 'the ones who return', les revenants, as we say in French. It is a nice word.

There is a double meaning in *gui* (歸), which is important to understand. First it is a place to return to because it is where I belong. Normally the *gui* (鬼) return to the earth. But if they cannot return to the earth, because the proper rites have not been fulfilled, they will go somewhere else. If they have a place to return to, helped by the correct rituals and offerings, they will not become malicious.

In this text, there is the idea of giving the spirit a place to return to – a family that will act as his descendants and make offerings on his behalf. Therefore the soul of the dead man will be happy and will not be a hungry hunting ghost – an idea which is very popular in China. So this strength is not only linked to the body, but to the soul of the deceased, and if the souls lose their way for one reason or another, and do not know where to go, they try to nourish themselves, to feed, and take something from the living, and they can become very dangerous ghosts.

Further in the text there is the question whether this man who died violently and suddenly would become a *gui* (鬼), a kind of spirit being.

> 'When Zichan went to the country of Jin, Zhao Jingzi asked him whether he could become a spiritual being (*wei gui* 為 鬼). Zichan answered that he could, saying: In a human life the first transformation is called the *po*. Once the *po* are produced, the *yang* aspect is called the *hun*.'

At the very beginning of life, most certainly during pregnancy, the *po* is actualized. Once the *po* is present the *hun* is able to manifest. This in fact fits very well with what we saw when we studied pregnancy and gestation [cf: Monkey Press 2007]; the first movement is always of the *yin* and the essences. If there is not a movement of the *yin* – of *yin qi* gathering together to create the very beginning of essences and form – there cannot be a specific expression of the *qi* and of the *yang*. In order to live and take form on earth, there must first be a condensation of essences, a place to gather and welcome the *qi*. As soon as the formation of the essences begins, the *yang*, or the *hun* aspect of the presence of heaven, is able to manifest itself. So the presence of heaven on earth needs this earthly aspect. This is the plan. That is not to say that the first is the most important, but that in the production of life on earth, this is the first movement. So first there is the *po*, which is the ability to have a human form, and it is because of this ability to have a human form, that a specific expression of *qi* is possible.

But we have to be careful when speaking of what comes first. If we speak of the possibility to form a new life on earth, the *yin* movement is first, because it expresses the receptivity of the earth without which nothing is possible. First we need the matrix to receive *qi* and to shelter transformations. But if we are speaking of a new life in the universe, heaven always comes first. Because without movement, without the *qi*, the will coming from heaven, nothing can happen either on earth or anywhere else. Heaven masters beginnings; it initiates all life and is ultimately responsible for what this form of life is – its original nature. In the text here, *po* are named first, and then the *hun*. In other texts, mainly ones written centuries later, the *hun* will come before the *po* in the development of the embryo and the foetus, as the representative of heaven. *Po* will come later as representative of earth. The *yin* movement is first on an earth which is already constituted. The basic idea is expressed here:

> 'In human life, the first transformation (the beginning, and the result of the transforming process of this beginning, *shi hua* 始 化) is called *po*; once the *po* are produced (*sheng* 生), the *yang* aspect is called *hun*.'
> 人 生 始 化 曰 魄 既 生 魄 陽 曰 魂
> *ren sheng shi hua yue po ji sheng po yang yue hun*

In this text it is very simple. There is nothing specific, no mention of seven *po* for example. (In fact the idea of numbers linked to the *hun* and the *po* appears later, not before the 4th and 3rd centuries BCE). The *hun* and *po* are not something that is put into a body, they are a potentiality – something to be developed. We can also see here that the *hun* are related to *yang* and not to heaven, so there is no idea of hierarchy.

'If there is an abundance of things and essences, then the *hun* and *po* are strong.'
用物精多則魂魄強
yong wu jing duo ze hun po qiang

'From this develop essence and understanding until there is the radiance of the spirits.'
是以有精爽至於神明
shi yi you jing shuang zhi yu shen ming

So from this ability to nourish oneself with the most pure and powerful aspects of things (essences, *jing* 精), the core of vitality, which is the *hun* and *po*, the body and mind, will be more and more powerful. Understanding and ability will develop, which will allow clarity of the mind and radiance of the spirits (*shen ming* 神命), which here suggests a kind of luminous intelligence. The text goes on:

'When an ordinary man or woman dies an ordinary death, the *hun* and *po* are able to hang about (on earth) and do evil and malicious things.'

When there is a violent death there can be disturbance and separation, a dislocation. It is similar to the action of *jing* (驚) to start with fright, where there is a separation, a partition, of blood and *qi*, *yin* and *yang*.

This is similar. When there is a sudden violent death, and especially if it takes you by surprise, there is the same kind of movement, which results in panic and disarray, and the souls don't know where to go. The *po*, which normally cannot leave the body, are forced out by this sudden violent aggressive shock. And they hang around and do evil – not because they want to – but because they are hungry. They are not in the right place. They do not know where the body is, or the essences that they are so used to. They are lost. This is probably the most ancient text that expresses this kind of thing.

This is also the reason why there are richly decorated 'straw dogs', or statues, at a funeral, the idea being that if there are some lost souls around, they might take up residence in these 'false' bodies and then they will be burned.

Here we are talking of the *po* and the *po* leaving the body because of severe shock. The *po* still have some strength, some kind of life, and a desire to find something to nourish them. So these kind of wandering souls are called hungry, and are calmed by offering them food. I don't know whether it is the same now, but when I was in Taiwan some 40 years ago they still had this kind of ritual, even in the city. There is a special festival in the spring, Qing Ming, when food is offered in the street to the hungry ghosts. There are also many similar Daoist rituals. When there are too many harmful influences around the village from these wandering souls, special rituals are performed, offering food and trying to give the lost souls a place to return to. There are also burial rituals; even if there is nothing to bury, there would still be a ritual burial to help the *po* return to the right place.

It is not the same with a natural death, when the *po* do not leave the body, though it may still be necessary to take some precautions. To be sure that the *po* will not leave, the orifices may be closed, traditionally by putting jade or rice in the mouth and even more specifically the anus, which is the 'door of the *po*' (*po men* 魄 門). If the *po* remain within the body and slowly dissolve back to the earth, then they will not become dangerous. This is a general idea, though there may be many variations.

Question: There seem to be many translations of *gui*, sometimes ghosts, sometimes spiritual beings – and that seems quite different.

You will find many different variations in the translation of *gui*. But they are essentially the spirits of the earth, and may have this potential to suck out your life. So to translate *gui* as spiritual beings is a bit misleading! But the *gui* can also be deities of the earth – spirits of the mountain, the marshes, rocks or ravines. This is very common. They are usually called *gui*, though some of them also have specific names. They are not necessarily bad, sometimes they are a good omen, but you always have to be a bit careful. It is a kind of spiritual force, a soul force, that we could possibly translate as spiritual beings, but this is also a translation for *shen* (神), and that can cause confusion. But ghost is maybe a bit limiting too. It is an earthly spirit. The text of the Zuozhuan continues:

> 'How much more in the case of Boyou, a descendent of Duke Mu, the grandson of Ziliang, the son of Zier, all ministers of the state, engaged in government for three generations. Zhang is not a great state, but a small insignificant one. But because his family had governed for three generations, his use of things must have been extensive, and his enjoyment of subtle essences abundant. Furthermore, his clan is large, and there was much to which he could cling. Is it not right that having died a violent death that he would become a ghost (*gui* 鬼)?'

Rituals at death

The first ritual which takes place after death is the summons of the soul (*zhao hun* 招魂). This is a very old ritual, and is an attempt to call back the *hun* to the body. If the *po* are still there, it is possible for the *hun* to return and reintegrate with the body, therefore avoiding death. There are examples in several civilizations, including those close to China, of shamanistic rituals to summon back the soul after death. The Yili, the Handbook of Rituals for Gentlemen, cites another ritual; in this case the death is of a person of high rank, but it could be anyone. And these rituals have been witnessed even in the 20th century.

'A soul summoner must take a suit of court robes formally worn by the deceased. And having first pinned the skirt and coat together he is to lay it over his left shoulder with the collar tucked into his belt. And in this manner setting a ladder against the front eaves at the east of the house, he is to mount up to the ridge of the roof and there facing northwards and stretching out the clothing to call out three times in a loud voice – Ho – such a one! Come back! Then he is to hand the clothes down from the eaves to another below, who is to receive them into a box, and carry it into the house, entering by way of the eastern steps. This other person, going into the house where the deceased lies, is to lay the clothing down upon the corpse. The summoner meanwhile must descend from the roof by the west end of the rear eaves.'

In the Songs of Chu (Chuci) there is a poem called the Summons of the Soul, Zhaohun (招魂), which is almost the same. The Songs of Chu are from the south, where there has always been a strong shamanic influence. And in the Liji, The Book of Rites, there is a similar kind of summons of the soul, calling back the *hun*, with a description which is very similar; going onto the roof of the house and calling back the soul.

> 'In death, they go to the rooftops and call out the name of the deceased in a long note, saying, 'come back, come back!' After this they fill the mouth with uncooked rice and make offerings of raw flesh. They look up to heaven and bury the body in the earth. The body and the *po* (*ti po* 體 魄) go down; the intelligence and *qi* (*zhi qi* 知 氣) ascend. Thus the dead are placed with their head to the north, while the living look towards the south. In all these matters the earliest practice is followed.'

There were also rites performed for the spirits of the ancestors, with offerings of meat, grains and liquor; music was played, and in this same chapter of the Book of Rites it says that attention must be paid to all of that, but also to the words of the ritual. There are prayers, but also a dialogue between the descendants and the deceased, with someone playing the role of the representative of the deceased and speaking for them. They make a kind of mediation on their behalf, speaking aloud, and describing what is happening with the spirits of the ancestors – whether they are happy, whether they eat well, etc. All that was part of the ritual, and it was very important to create that kind of communication.

All the rituals, offerings, music, speech and so on, all the formulas of invocation and blessings, were a way to help the spirits above descend and those below to ascend. Through that it is possible to maintain the harmony and good conduct of all members of the family, so that everybody is living in the right place and with beneficial influences.

'By all these offerings and rituals, we rejoice the soul of the deceased and realize through that the union between the living and the dead'

In this kind of ritual, *hun* and *po* could be summoned from above and from below, each with a specific ritual, in order to be reunited for the time of the ritual.

Book of Rites, Liji

There is a very famous passage in the Liji (chapter Jiyi) which shows the difference between *gui* (鬼) and *shen* (神). It is a dialogue which is supposed to have taken place between Confucius and a disciple:

'They are always speaking of *gui* and *shen*, but I do not know what these words mean.'

Confucius replies: 'The *qi* have a spirit-like (*shen* 神) nature, and the *po* belong to the *gui* (鬼). To reunite the spirits of heaven and the spirits of earth is the supreme filial piety.

'All that is living must die, and when one dies, one goes back to the earth. That is what is called *gui*. The bones and the flesh are dead and go down and are buried, in order to become the soil of the fields. But the *qi* of the deceased spreads out and rises in the heights to become glorious and full of light (*ming* 明).'

Here the *po* are associated with the *qi* rather than the *hun*. In the Liji we have already seen the *hun* alluded to by the expression *hun qi* (魂 氣),

and again as intelligent *qi* (*zhi qi* 知氣) – the *qi* full of the capacity to know, to understand and capable of building consciousness.

In the lower part of the Mawangdui funeral banner (see frontispiece and cover image), there are seven beings representing the seven *po*. There are dishes and bowls containing offerings of grain and meat around them. There is also a vapour which ascends to the three *hun*, following the deceased on her way to heaven. The imagery in the banner is very similar to these texts, and shows that the rituals were a part of normal life.

There is a double offering, something to attract the *hun* and something to attract the *po*, giving the soul a place to return to. In another chapter, when the liquor enters the earth, the *po* are able to come back and participate in the ritual. The smell of the burning of sacrificed animals and the feeling and music attract the *hun*. So there is something to attract the spirits from above and from below, the spirits of the *yin* and of the *yang*. It is necessary to search for the *hun* and the *po*, whether they are in the depths of the soil or full of light above.

Qi and *hun* are both formless, ascending and circulating in heaven. For this reason, *hun* are traditionally referred to as the '*qi* soul', while *po* are the 'blood soul'. Here the blood represents substance, the form aspect of the couple *xue qi* (血氣). This couple of blood and *qi* is older than the theory of medicine, and in classical non-medical texts was used to speak of the vitality, including both corporeal and spiritual or mental aspects.

It is important to understand that in ancient non-medical texts, when speaking of the '*qi* soul' as the *hun*, and the 'blood soul' as the *po*, it is to refer to the pattern of the *qi* as *yang*, heaven, formless, insubstantial, incorporeal, and the blood as *yin*, earth, substance, form, body and flesh. In this case, *hun* and *qi* are of the same nature, as are *po* and blood. In the medical texts, we see a different association. The *hun*, through their link with the liver are associated with liver blood, but this is a *yin* (blood) and *yang* (*hun*) relationship. It is the same thing for the *po* (*yin*) and the *qi* (*yang*) of the lung.

Baihutong

In the Baihutong, Discussion of the White Tiger Hall, a book from the 1st century CE on the correct interpretation of the classics attributed to Ban Gu (32-92 CE), there is the question in chapter 8, 'What are the *hun* and *po*?' The answer is as follows:

> 'The *hun* are like clouds. They are the *qi* of the young *yang* (*shao yang* 少 陽) and therefore move without stopping.'

The character for *hun* (魂) expresses this idea of circulating continually. It is a movement towards the exterior. Young *yang* is the spring, which is full of *qi* and power, and with the ability to create motion and rise. This type of *qi* will become associated with the *qi* of the spring and become the most powerful expression of the *yang* and its movement upward and outward, as represented by the functional activity of the liver.

> 'The *po* (魄) presses urgently, it is attached and clings on. It is the *qi* of young *yin* (*shao yin* 少 陰), which are in the image of metal and stone, they cling to human beings without moving, without going elsewhere.'

They cannot travel like the *hun*, and in the body they produce the pressing urge to eat and to breathe, and all that is necessary for the continuation of the life of the body. There is a lot of play on words in this text. *Po* (魄) is explained by another character *po* (迫) which has the meaning of pressing urgently.

The character *yun* (芸) contains that of clouds (*yun* 云) with vegetation, and is a character with several meanings: one is to weed, and it is explained as weeding out what is not pure, weeding out the impurities of one's nature, behaviour and so on. The *po* are compared with whiteness, (*bai* 白), which also means to whiten or to make pure. To whiten someone is to declare him not guilty. This is quite a common expression. In Chinese, the character for white also means to be pure and clear, and also the verb to clear – to make void and empty. It suggests that the *po* are able to cleanse feelings and emotions, to make them empty and appropriate. It is quite common to have this kind of play on words in the texts of this time.

SUMMARY

We can see in these early texts that the *hun* and *po* enable the initiation of human life – they allow the basic movement of life. And if life is ruled in such a way that the *hun* develop in the likeness of heaven and all that belongs to heaven, then not only will there be a balanced temperament, a peaceful mind, a kind of accuracy of intelligence, and skill, with speech, art, writing, creativity, imagination and so on – but this *hun* will also be ready to merge and become a spirit of heaven. Then of course the individual will no longer exist. The *po* on the other hand will merge with the decomposing body in the earth and return to the power of earth. But there are many opportunities to get lost, especially with a violent death, and when travelling towards heaven, the way is never easy. There is no question of an immortal soul. The soul will last as long as there is enough strength to survive as a specific spirit. Offerings help the *hun* to continue to be what they are, to remain an individual *hun*. If there are no more offerings, and if there is still a lot of strength they could become erratic, but usually there is simply an extinction. If the offerings decline, the power declines, the memory declines. And what is left – something in heaven. No one really knows what it is.

So this is just a general overview of what is found in the classical texts on the *hun* and the *po*. What we see in the medical texts is of course based on that, but in each kind of text, whether Daoist or Buddhist and so on, *hun* and *po* are seen in a specific way. There may be difficulties if these different levels of understanding are confused.

The number of the hun and po

Question: Can you say something about the numbers associated with the *hun* and *po*?

This came quite a bit later, and is certainly not found in the earliest texts. Numbers were not given before the 3rd century BCE, when they have a specific symbolic value. We have seen that the *hun* are linked with the *qi*, and the number three is the proper number for the *qi*. The *po* could be linked to feeling, or strength of life and vitality, and the number seven is the number of the vital strength, but this is not a very convincing argument! It is one possible explanation, but there are other numbers which would fit just as well.

Three plus seven makes ten, and that is important. The total number of human souls should be ten because ten is the number of humanity. That can be seen in many ways, for example the duration of pregnancy in the human species is ten lunar months. Human life is normally 100 years (10 x 10). Ten is a number of perfection, in Chinese it is written 十. In very archaic writing and bronze inscriptions it is a vertical stroke. It may allude to four around a centre – a centre able to rule the four directions, which implies a totality of space.

There is a later interpretation that the vertical axis represents heaven and the horizontal axis represents earth and that these unite in the number ten. Also ten is the last number because there is a specific character for numbers one to ten; eleven being ten plus one. Apart from one to ten, there are specific characters only for one hundred, one thousand and ten thousand. So the character ten (*shi* 十) can have the meaning of something total and perfect.

The human being is seen as the most perfect being in the universe, living between heaven and earth, and expressing within the body the totality of the cosmos. So ten is the most convenient number for human beings, but this is, of course, the opinion of human beings – this text is not written by ants or leopards! So it was considered necessary to have a total of ten souls. If there must be a total of ten, and if the *hun* is linked with the *qi* and is therefore associated with the number three, then the other number must be seven. Of course there may be other explanations, but if you must have ten, maybe three plus seven is the best option – none of the others work so well! I know of no texts with other numbers.

In Daoist texts there is often a distinction made between the three levels of the *hun*, or seven variations of the *po*. The three levels of *hun* are often related to the three divisions of the body – the lower, middle and upper *dan tian* (丹 田). In some later Daoist texts, a differentiation is often made between the three levels of the *hun*. And sometimes there are pictures of the seven *po*, but these are very specific religious texts. Seven is often related to the vital spirits, the vitality, and to the tiger. The tigress has seven months of pregnancy.

Three and seven are often used in the Book of Rites to refer to some kind of transition. When someone dies, the relatives mourn for three years; three months after a wedding the wife will return to see her mother; after a child is born it is put on the earth for three days before taking care of it. So three is a symbolic number, which represents a kind of transformational cycle. Seven very often represents an initial completion, nine is the full completion, and with ten everything is integrated within a unity.

In the ten months of pregnancy, in the third month the embryo becomes a foetus, and in the seventh month, there is the first completion. After that there is movement and quickening. Of course there may be other reasons, but in Chinese civilization, three and seven are good numbers, and certainly it may be important that they are prime numbers.

HUN AND PO IN MEDICAL TEXTS

Lingshu chapter 8

In the classical medical texts, we will begin with Neijing Lingshu chapter 8, which is a fundamental chapter for many reasons. It is important to remember that even within the medical texts it is possible to find many different kinds of uses of *hun* and *po*. In the first part of this chapter, the *hun* and the *po* are mentioned with the essences and spirits, *jing shen* (精 神), as allowing human life to manifest itself and to build an individual concept of self, which is the heart. The intent (*yi* 意) and the will (*zhi* 志) follow the heart in the text.

> 'The coming forth of living beings (life, *sheng* 生)
> is called essences.
> 故 生 之 來 謂 之 精
> *gu sheng zhi lai wei zhi jing*

> 'The embrace of two essences,
> is called spirits.
> 兩 精 相 搏 謂 之 神
> *liang jing xiang bo wei zhi shen*

> 'That which follows the spirits in their going and coming
> is called *hun*.
> 隨 神 往 來 者 謂 之 魂
> *sui shen wang lai zhe wei zhi hun*

'That which associates with the essences
in their entering and exiting is called *po*.
並精而出入者謂之魄
bing jing er chu ru zhe wei zhi po

'When something takes charge of the being,
that is called the heart (*xin* 心).'
所以任物者謂之心
suo yi ren wu zhe wei zhi xin

A strong link is made here between the *hun* and the spirits on the one hand and between the *po* and the essences on the other. This text is part of a presentation of the essences and spirits, the vital spirits, with the essences seen as the core of vitality within any kind of substance, and that fits very well with the functioning of the *po*. The *hun* follow, and also have to become like the *shen*, the spirits of heaven. The essences come first in this text, because in order to speak of a living being there must first be essences. There must be a *yin* concentration, which is represented here by the essences. Several times within the medical texts you will find that in speaking of a living being, there must first be essences; the beginning of life always indicates that essences are present. In Lingshu chapter 10 it says that at the beginning of human life the essences are perfectly composed.

Life is made by a meeting, a coming together, and it is through the essences, and because of the specific nature of human essences, which are naturally pure and clear, that this meeting is possible. The refined quality of the essences attracts the spirits of heaven; as soon as essences come together, and begin to compose something – in the text the embrace of two essences – there is the possibility for the spirits to come and so to enable the formation of a human being. The embrace of the essences may be the union of father and mother, or *yin* and *yang*, or heaven and earth through the father and mother. This is the very basis of life seen in terms of *jing* and *shen*.

The text of Lingshu chapter 8 closely relates the *hun* to the spirits:

> 'That which follows (*sui* 隨) the spirits (*shen* 神) in their going and coming is called *hun*.'

There are two important things here. One is a kind of obedience. *Sui* (隨) is to follow faithfully, like a lady in waiting. The Mawangdui funeral banner depicts the three *hun* as the ladies in waiting of the deceased, the Marchioness of Dai. The *hun* follow faithfully, and they have to obey. Life on earth simply has to follow the natural order, to model itself on the way of heaven and everything will be perfect.

Another interesting point is that the *hun* 'follow the spirits in their going and coming', and that is quite different from the *po*, which 'associate with the essences in their exiting and entering'. To exit and to enter, we need openings – doors, gates or passages. But to go and come it is not necessary to have an opening. This idea is quite common in the medical texts but also elsewhere. The proper movement of the spirits is to go and come, quite freely, and the text suggests that the *hun* have that kind of freedom. They do not need openings, apertures or orifices to enter or leave the body. By nature they rise up and one of their favourite places to leave is through the sutures of the skull, where, in children, the fontanels are still open. They naturally have this movement upwards, so it is natural for them to leave through the top of the head. They are able to go and come back, as in dreams or meditation, or in some kind of trance or ecstatic state.

When the *hun* are not present, the body is motionless and there is no sign of life, just a kind of imperceptible *qi*, because the person is not dead. We can see this at the beginning of Zhuangzi chapter 2. The *hun* may go on what is called 'the wandering of the souls', or 'the ecstatic journey', which is a spiritual journey where the *hun* leave the body of the adept. But it is important to be an adept, one who knows how to leave and to come back, for if you are unable to return you will die. The *hun* are able to wander in heaven and meet whoever is in heaven, with purity and accuracy, intelligence, and universal knowledge – even outside space and time – encountering other spiritual beings. And then they come back. This kind of dreaming, or visioning, was documented in ancient times, and if there is no imbalance within the soul, it is possible to meet with others. It is also mentioned in Zhuangzi chapter 2, as we have seen, that during sleep or rest, the *hun* may meet together, or 'go visiting'. This suggests that they visit other spirits, such as the spirits of the ancestors (as in Confucius' dreams) or deities (as when dreaming in a temple) – or in fact make contact with any other spirit able to inspire or comfort them.

So the *hun* are capable of this kind of movement. They are not prisoners of the body, and as part of me, they are everything that is linked with what has no form (*wu xing* 無 形) – movement, intelligence, cleverness, knowledge, sensitivity, imagination, spirituality, creativity, dreams, contemplation and so on. All of this is necessary in order to have reason and clarity of mind, which is illuminated by the light of the spirits (*shen ming* 神 明). It is possible to be very imaginative and very rational, but it is also possible to be very imaginative and not based in reality, which can lead to madness. This functioning of the heart/mind begins with what we call will (*zhi* 志) and intent (*yi* 意).

The *po* are very different; they are associated with the essences which are the vitality within the body, and for this reason they cannot leave the body, they cannot exist outside the body. They are closely linked to substance and to leave the body they have to go through openings, to exit and to enter, for example through the mouth or the anus. At death, these orifices are blocked. During life, the *po* are responsible for all the instinctive vital movements, the pressing urges, as is said in the Baihutong; the feelings and reactions which are sentient. And that is the reason why *po* is sometimes translated as the sentient souls.

The text of Lingshu 8 goes on to say that it is because we have this power of the essences and spirits, *hun* and *po* within us, that we are able to have a heart – which is the self. And when there is a heart, it is possible to take charge of one's life:

'When something takes charge of the being, that is called the heart'.

The heart, in this context, has to be understood as the unity of heaven and earth, *hun* and *po*, spirit and body within an individual. My heart is, and remains, my life. It is the unity of life, the harmony of the five *zang*, which ensures good physiological functioning, as well as the accuracy and discernment of the mind. When the heart stops beating, it is the end of this unity and the end of the present life. When I am able to take charge of my life, it is not only that this double power of the *hun* and *po* have enabled me to live, but now I am responsible for the quality, the purity and the strength of my own life. Depending on the life I have been given, and the way I am able to concentrate and assimilate good and pure essences, to have good thoughts and few desires, I am able to transform my *hun* into glorious and luminous spirits, and my *po* will be at rest, satisfied, with nothing urging or pressing. So my life is quiet and my death is just a movement of *yang* and a recall of *yin*. It is simply the *yang* movement towards heaven and the *yin* movement towards earth. The power and purity of both components, heavenly and earthly, spiritual and bodily, make up the power and purity of the heart/mind, of the self and of the individual life.

The heart here is more than one of the five *zang* – it is the unity of an individual life. It is not only one of the five *zang* – it is the oneness of the five *zang*. The heart is the individual self, the ability to take responsibility for the individual life. So how is it possible to form the heart? Through the vital spirits, the essences, spirits, *hun* and *po*, I have heaven and earth within me, and I am able to build the heart of a human being, and as a human being, I am responsible for my life. Being responsible for my life is the same thing as being responsible for the *hun* and *po*.

The *yi* (意) and the *zhi* (志), the intent and the will, also appear in this first part of the presentation of Lingshu chapter 8. Both characters contain the heart (*xin* 心) within them, because will and intent are the will and intent of the heart. These five characters (*shen* 神, *hun* 魂, *po* 魄, *yi* 意, *zhi* 志) are the five aspects of spirit (*wu shen* 五 神). The *shen* (神) which are related to the heart are the only aspect of spirit to descend from above, and in this context, *hun* and *po* are related to the emergence of human life on earth, between the instigation of heaven and the acceptance of earth; *yi* (意) and *zhi* (志) are related to the human heart. The five *shen* also represent the three levels of heaven, earth and humanity. These three different levels are represented within the five *shen*, with *hun* and *po* being the souls at the very depths of human life, and intent and will more dependent on the self, the heart/mind, and the product of that. At death, the heart disappears, and as 'I' disappear, so the intent and the will as such disappear. The *hun* and *po* have some kind of destiny after death, as do the *shen*; the *shen* are heaven and the *hun* may become *shen*, but the *yi* and the *zhi* are at a different level.

There is also another way to look at it. Each of the five inner organs (*zang* 臟) needs to have its own spirit, because the five *zang* are the five ways in which life expresses itself. There is a kind of spiritual power behind each of the five *zang*, which gives its own characteristics and activity to life at the most superior level of the being – the mind, the spirit, the soul – or whatever words we may choose to use in English. In this case, each of the five spirits is related to one organ, and this is seen in the medical texts (and sometimes in other texts), the heart being linked with the *shen*, the liver with the *hun*, the lung with the *po*, the spleen with the *yi* and the kidneys with the *zhi*. Though the kidneys may be linked with either the will or the essences in different contexts.

As soon as there is a group of five, this implies *wu xing* (五 行), the five aspects of *qi*, or the five ways for the *qi* to behave, to move, to act and react when within form on earth. In this case it is only possible to consider each in relation to the five, so we would see *hun* as linked to the moving and rising action of wood, and the *po* as linked to the descending and concentrating action of metal, and by extension the *hun* to the liver and the *po* to the lung. We will look at this later, but this is not quite the same as the more general way we have seen the *hun* previously; the relationship between the liver and the wood *qi* is not quite the same thing as the *hun* being the heavenly part of my individual life.

As we have seen, the *hun* and *po* create human life here on earth. They are the meeting of heaven and earth within a human form – within a form taken on earth. There must always be something coming from heaven, which in this case is the *shen*, and the *shen* are this kind of light, or the ability that we all have to become *shen*-like. In my life I hope to become *shen*-like, and that is another way of saying that the *hun* follow the *shen*. If I nourish the *po*, taking care of the needs of the body, my body will be at peace. I take care of the good balance between *hun* and *po* and heaven and earth within me, and I direct that from my heart. My heart responds by the creation of the mental disposition; the mind is never blank, there are always tendencies and attachments, ideas and desires, and an inner disposition and mentality expressed by the intent and the will. 'Will' is the will to live, the drive of life, and 'intent' is the ability to build thought, decision, desires and so on. This building of the mental world depends on the disposition of the heart. It is an expression of the heart/mind, and so it is not at the same level as the *hun* and the *po*. It is possible to speak of these three levels. The hierarchy of *hun* and *po* does not exist as such between *yi* and *zhi*, they are in more of a continuity. One is not in a more prevalent position than the other.

When we consider the five spirits, we cannot see the *hun* in quite the same way as we saw them previously; they become more the expression of the movement of *qi* which is linked to wood, to spring, to the liver and so on. We find in the Wuxing Taiyi, the Great Explanation of the Five Elements, that the *hun* are the *qi* of wood, the *shen* the *qi* of fire, will the *qi* of earth, the *po* the *qi* of metal and the essences the *qi* of water. This kind of variation is often found within the different texts. The *hun* communicate with the eyes, the *shen* with the tongue, the *po* with the nose, etc. This kind of association is found not only in the medical texts, but in all kinds of cosmological organization by five. There may easily be misunderstanding, because it is difficult to know the level that the text is coming from. So the understanding of the *hun* in the various classical texts that we have seen is different from the meaning in this kind of text, which refers to the five movements of *qi*; this is quite a different thing, and if we try to stretch the *wu xing* theory too far, or in the wrong context, we soon come across difficulties. Nevertheless, there is always a relationship and continuity between these various levels of understanding of the *hun*.

In Lingshu chapter 8, there is an awareness of these different levels;

the first part of the text is on quite a general level, but it also introduces the five *shen*. The second part of the text is more specific and defines the five *shen* according to the five movements of *qi*.

'The liver stores the blood, the blood is the dwelling place of the *hun*. …The lung stores the *qi*, the *qi* are the dwelling place of the *po*.'

The liver is full of blood, and is the dwelling place of the *hun*, because of the relationship between the liver, the wood, *shao yang*, the spring and the rising movement of liver *qi*. The *qi* of the liver are powerful. There is a natural rising movement, which is always in danger of rising up too strongly. There is a similar relationship between the *po* and the lung, as the lung is related to autumn, metal, the pressing down movement. We saw this urgency and pressure previously in relation to the *po*, and of course this can also be linked with the lung. This was most probably the basis for the earliest associations.

So the liver is full of blood and blood is the liquid which comes from the heart – full of the presence of the spirits, the *shen*. There is a relationship between the *shen* and the *hun* through the blood, and this gives the liver its special function in the balance of the mind – in the management of emotions, feelings and passions, and its importance in the function of intelligence, the ability to speak, imagination, dreams and so on. All that is related to the liver, specifically the blood of the liver, and is readily associated with the *hun*; the liver is a suitable place for the *hun* to dwell. The *hun* participate in forming the spiritual quality of the blood and the balance of the mind. When the '*hun* are not kept in their dwelling place', there are symptoms of too much dreaming. The substance of the blood is able to balance and hold the volatile *hun*, which are always ready to take off! It is difficult to know whether the mental function of the liver is the reason for it being linked with the *hun*, or whether the link of the liver with the *hun* is the reason for its association with the mind.

We can also see these relationships between the *po* and the lung. Though of course, the lung does not work in the same way as the liver. The liver is much more involved with psychology, with the mind and the spirits than the lung. All the *zang* have some involvement with the mind, but at a general level, the liver has a more obvious connection. The lung is closely linked with this kind of pressing urge for life – which is seen clearly in the breathing. We cannot help but breathe, and it is a good example of the vital force at work within the body, which has nothing to do with mental ability. But it is possible to breathe well or badly, and it is possible to regulate the breathing. Through the link between the lung and the *po*, it is possible to see the vital, instinctive movement of life. The baby's first cry comes from the lung and is an expression of the movement of life. If prevented from breathing, even the wisest of men will struggle with all his physical force to begin breathing again.

We have already seen the strong association between the *hun* and the *qi*, but in Lingshu chapter 8 the 'blood is the dwelling place of the *hun*' and the '*qi* is the dwelling place of the *po*'. There can be misunderstandings here, but, as we have seen previously, it is usually due to a mixing of contexts and different levels of thinking. The link stated in Lingshu chapter 8 is specific. It is not between *hun* and blood and *po* and *qi*, but between the *hun* and the blood of the liver, and the *po* and the *qi* of the lung. There is a *yin yang* relationship between *hun* and *po*, *qi* and blood, and consequently between *hun* and blood, *po* and *qi*, which both maintains them and prevents their dissemination and departure.

The blood of the liver, in the lower heater, moors the *hun* as the *yin* stabilize and keep the *yang*. The *qi* of the lung, in the upper heater, balance the *po*, which always have a tendency to press down, to descend to the earth, just as the *yang* prevents the falling and sinking of vital substances. Life always appears and is maintained by these working couples, which are able to build a constant and harmonious relationship. When the relationship no longer holds, the partners separate, the blood no longer circulates because its embrace with the *qi* has ended; *hun* and *po* are no longer in unity, they disentangle, which means death. When the working couples are in balance, the *hun* do not leave prematurely and the *po* do not return to the earth; they remain embodied.

We can understand that some pathology of the blood of the liver and the *qi* of the lung may be related to the *hun* and *po*. But there is not a pathology of the *hun* and *po* as such. Here in the medical texts it is more a pathology of the blood of the liver and the *qi* of the lung. It is a pathology that can be analysed according to *yin yang* or the five phases as expressed in the five *zang*. A *yin yang* imbalance of the liver or the lung will result, for instance, in a deficiency of the blood of the liver or a weakness of the *qi* of the lung with an associated result in the *hun* or the *po*.

Pathology in Lingshu chapter 8:

> 'When the liver is prey to sadness and affliction, one is moved at the centre, then the *hun* are injured. The *hun* injured, one becomes mad (*kuang* 狂) and forgetful (*wang* 忘), and there is no more vitality (essences, *jing* 精). In this situation the genitals (*yin* 陰) contract, the musculature (*jin* 筋) cramps, the flanks on both sides can no longer rise. The body hair becomes brittle, and one has all the signs of premature death. One dies in autumn.'

'When the lung is prey to boundless elation and joy, the *po* are injured, when the *po* are injured one becomes mad (*kuang* 狂). With this madness the intent (*yi* 意) knows no-one, the skin shrivels and wrinkles. The body hair becomes brittle and one has signs of premature death. One dies in summer.'

Here the *hun* represent the wood movement of *qi* in the spiritual and mental world. It is the same thing with the *po* and the lung. The *po* express the movement of *qi* proper to metal and the lung, at the level of the most subtle and powerful aspects of life.

The pathology presented is not so much a pathology of the *hun* and *po*, but more a pathology of the movement of the life force within the liver and lung. What is interesting in Lingshu chapter 8 is that in both cases, when the *hun* and *po* souls are injured, we become mad, which is not the case for the other injuries referred to in the text. The madness is not the same; with the *po*, there is an injury to the very basic functioning of the lung and to metal; the intent knows no-one. It is a kind of dementia. In the case of the *hun*, there is a lack of blood and vitality, with a kind of shrivelling up of the muscles; with the lung, the skin is affected. This is typical of this kind of classification by five. The text concludes:

'This being so, one who wishes to use needles must examine attentively the way the patient presents themselves, to perceive the preservation or disappearance of the vital spirits (*jing shen* 精 神), the *hun* and *po*, and whether the inner disposition (*yi* 意) is favourable or unfavourable. If those five are injured, the needle cannot treat.'

In Lingshu chapter 8, the spiritual aspects are presented as five, in order to show how life is guided by the emotions.

HUN AND PO IN OTHER MEDICAL TEXTS

Hun and *po* are presented as aspects of the five *shen* in many medical texts, as for example Suwen chapter 23 or Lingshu chapter 78. In relation to the five *zang*, the heart treasures (stores, *cang* 藏) the *shen*, the lung the *po*, the liver the *hun*, the spleen the *yi* and the kidneys either the will (*zhi* 志) in Suwen chapter 23, or in Lingshu chapter 78 the essences and the will. The five *zang* organs are differentiated from the six *fu* organs as being able to regulate everything that relates to the spirits and the mind, as opposed to the six *fu* which are more related to the substantial, corporeal aspect of life. For instance in Lingshu chapter 52:

> 'The five *zang* (臟) are for treasuring (*cang* 藏) the essences and spirits (vital spirits, *jing shen* 精 神) the *hun* and the *po* (魂 魄), while the six *fu* (六 府) are for receiving liquids and grains and for circulating (*xing* 行) and transforming (*hua* 化) substances.'

The substances here are those circulating in the digestive tract, and we can see that when it is a question of division between *zang* and *fu*, the *fu* are related to substances, the body form, digestion and all that proceeds from digestion, and the spirits and the mind are related to the *zang*. This is also found in Lingshu chapter 47:

> 'The five *zang* are for treasuring (*cang* 藏) the vital spirits (*jing shen* 精 神), blood and *qi* (*xue qi* 血 氣), *hun* and *po* (魂 魄). The six *fu* are for transforming (*hua* 化) liquids and grains and for circulating (*xing* 行) body fluids (*jin ye* 津 夜).'

Here *hun* and *po* are both in the category of the formless; they are the spirits animating the *qi* of the five *zang*. In both Lingshu chapters 52 and 47, the five *shen* are not given as such; there are simply essences and spirits, *hun* and *po*. Lingshu chapter 47 includes the blood and *qi*, which is the way in which spirits and awareness pervade the being.

There are other texts that differentiate *hun* and *po* according to their relationships with the liver and lung. For example in Suwen chapter 9:

> 'The liver is the root of extreme cessation. It is the residence of the *hun*. Its flourishing aspect is the nails, its full power is in the muscular forces, it is for the invigoration of blood and *qi*. Its taste is sour, its colour is azure, it is *shao yang* within the *yang*. It has a free and easy communication with the *qi* of the spring.'

Extreme cessation here is the opposite of the surging of energy in the springtime, which is proper to the good functioning of the liver. This kind of surge of life also suggests a good functioning of the muscles and the circulation. The *hun* are always moving the *yang*, so will also be exhausted first. Exhaustion is always seen first in that which is able to display the greatest movement – which is the liver. That is the reason why the liver is here called the root of extreme cessation.

In Suwen chapter 9 the *hun* are associated with the liver, the *shao yang*, the invigoration of blood and *qi*, and with all the movement of the body made through the muscular forces. At the same time it keeps some characteristics of the *hun*, but always under the specific aspect of the liver and wood *qi*.

> 'The lung is the root of the *qi*, the place of the *po*, its flourishing aspect is in the body hair, the power of its fullness is in the skin, it is the great *yin* within the *yang*, it is in free communication with the autumn *qi*.'

The *po* are linked with the lung, within this context of the *yin*, the autumn, and the very power of the *yin* movement of *qi* – descending, concentrating, going down, etc.

Within these texts, there is an understanding that *hun* and *po* are also linked with the *jing shen* (精 神), and sometimes with the *shen qi* (神 氣), which is the *qi* that is able to support the spirits and make the spirits present throughout the being. In this way, the *hun* and *po* are linked with the manifestation of the self, through the heart and also through the eyes – the eyes being the messenger of the heart. They are linked with the heart, as the heart is the centre of life and the place where the best essences of all the organs gather to nourish life. This is often compared to a kingdom, where the emperor is in the centre and receives tributes from all over the land, in order to be nourished by the best from each area. This is not only because he can do this, but because it is recognized as the best way to maintain the emperor as the heart of the country, to encourage the ability to govern well, and bring peace and benevolent influences to the whole empire. So the best produce of each territory comes to the emperor. In the same way, the best of the essences produced by the five *zang* come to the heart, to sustain the blood, which is not merely a body fluid, but represents the substance of life – blood and *qi* being not only the circulation of blood, but the visible aspect of the subtle workings of the entirety of life.

Lingshu chapter 80

'The essences and *qi* of the five *zang* and six *fu* all rise up to pour into the eyes and build the essences able to sustain the eyesight.'

Here 'the eyes' includes all the inner workings of the brain, which contribute to vision, and this is at the level of physical maintenance and protection, as well as at the level of the spirits. This is the reason why the text then says:

> 'The eyes are the essences of the five *zang* and the six *fu*, the place of constant nutrition (*ying* 營) and defence (*wei* 衛), *hun* and *po*. In the eyes, *qi* able to sustain the spirits is produced. This is the reason why when the spirits are tired, *hun* and *po* dissipate, will and intent are in disorder… there is no more transportation and the vision is no longer normal, essences and spirits, *hun* and *po* dissipate (*san* 散) and are no longer able to join together. This is called disarray.'

This is a slightly different way to see *hun* and *po*, here they represent the functioning of the liver and the lung at the spiritual level, as well as the common work of all the five *zang* to produce the reality of mental and spiritual life – which includes what we call the vital spirits, *hun* and *po*, intent and will. Everything present in the heart is also present in the eyes, including that which is able to nourish and protect (*ying wei* 營 衛). If we are not able to maintain a good relationship between all that makes up the mind and the spirits, not only is vision no longer normal, but the mind is in disarray. I no longer know where I am and I no longer know who I am. It is a kind of crisis of the self, related to the eyes, which in turn are related to the heart and brain.

The greatest danger for the *hun* and *po* is that they dissipate. We might say that this is more likely for the *hun*, but if the *hun* dissipate, the *po* are powerless. This scattering of the *hun* can create a disruption of the relationship between the *hun* and *po*. It is most important to avoid this dissipation (*san* 散).

Lingshu chapter 9

In Lingshu chapter 9 a situation is described where the patient is very agitated, unable to settle or even to be approached.

'Stay quiet in a peaceful place, observe the signs of the coming and going of the spirits (*shen wang lai* 神 往 來). Close windows and doors, so that *hun* and *po* do not dissipate (*bu san* 不 散). Concentrate your mind, (*zhuan yi* 專 意) unify your spirit (*yi shen* 一 神) so that essences and *qi* (*jing qi* 精 氣) distribute themselves correctly.

'When no human noise reaches the ears, the essences (*jing* 精) are gathered; and thus the spirits (*shen* 神), being in unity (oneness), the will (*zhi* 志) is present in the needle. The needle is inserted in the surface area and remains a while, manipulated with delicacy and at the surface, in order to move the spirits. As soon as the *qi* arrives, stop.'

We must try to help the patient come back to themselves, so that the needles will have someone to address. The needles address the person, not simply the body. It may be through the body, but there has to be someone to react to the signals given by the needles. If there is a scattering of the mind, of the *hun* and *po*, the patient is agitated and unable to settle down and be present – like a ghost, a shadow of the real person. We have to try to calm them down; there must be no noise, nothing that might distract the mind.

Hun and *po* are one way to speak of the individuality, the ability of the person to be centred in their life. *Hun* and *po* are the very basis of this – maintaining and sustaining individual life. If the *hun* and *po* are scattered, I am not necessarily dead but I have no real awareness. I need to allow my heart to receive and to answer, because without that presence of awareness, the treatment is almost useless. The state of the mind and the spirits creates disorder in the blood and *qi*, so it is very difficult to help. First we must try to calm the patient, and help them to settle down, to enable some kind of concentration, so that the spirits can be present and the person more aware of themselves. Then there will be more order in the essences and *qi*, and the message from the needle will have a way to affect the person.

Of course, the practitioners themselves must also concentrate and not let the *hun* and *po*, the mind and attention, be distracted. They must remain rooted. With this firm embrace of *hun* and *po*, which must be firmly rooted in one's own life there is a union and harmony of heaven and earth. This is of course the same for all treatment, and is also found in rituals – before performing a rite one must concentrate, purify oneself and be ready to do something effectively.

Lingshu chapter 47

In Lingshu chapter 47 there is the same view of *hun* and *po*, with the idea of gathering, avoiding dispersion, collecting and putting together.

'Humans, having blood and *qi*, essences and spirits, receive life from them. They ensure the regular movement between nature (*xing* 性) and destiny (*ming* 命). The meridians (*jing mai* 經 脈) make blood and *qi* circulate (*xing* 行), maintain *yin* and *yang*, moisten the muscular forces and the bones and allow the proper functioning of the joints. The defensive *qi* warm up the flesh and by passing through their separations (*fen rou* 分 肉) give their power to the layers of the skin, smooth the *cou li* (the texture of the skin 腠 理), directing openings and closings (of the pores, *kai he* 開 闔). Will and intent (*zhi yi* 志 意) are what direct the vital spirits, gather *hun* and *po*, regulate hot and cold and harmoniously blend (*he* 和) elation and anger (*xi nu* 喜 怒).'

It may seem strange that will and intent direct life in this way, but once there is a heart, a self, something that can take charge of human life, then there is individual responsibility for the quality of the vital spirits, *hun* and *po*. They are directly connected with the inner disposition of the heart, which we may call *zhi yi* (志 意), will and intent. This is not to say that they are superior, but once there is a functioning being, everything is directed through the heart, and it is through the individual behaviour, the way each individual lives their own life, that vital spirits are built and strength and vitality are given to the *hun* and *po*.

Will and intent direct the vital spirits, gather *hun* and *po*, regulate hot and cold and harmoniously blend elation and anger. Hot and cold are the external *qi* influences that have to be regulated by the way that we live our lives, and elation and anger, here representing all the emotions, are the inner threats to the correct movement of *qi* and must be balanced too.

'When will and intent are in harmony then the vital spirits (*jing shen* 精 神) are concentrated and correct, *hun* and *po* are not dissipated, regret and anger (*hui nu* 悔 怒) do not arise, the five *zang* do not receive perverse influences. …This is the normal equilibrium of a human being.'

Lingshu chapter 54

'The Yellow Emperor asked: What are the spirits (*shen* 神)?

'Qi Bo replied: When blood and *qi* are harmoniously composed, nutrition and defence circulating and communicating freely, the five *zang* are perfectly achieved so that the *qi* is able to support the spirits to dwell in the heart, *hun* and *po* possess all their capacities – this perfect achievement is a human being.'

It is interesting that the question is about the spirits, and the answer concerns the perfect human being, which is, of course, to be spirit-like. And how are we to be spirit-like? With the blood and *qi*, nutrition and defence, the five *zang*, the *qi* sustaining the spirits, and with the *hun* and *po* fulfilling their potential, they are able to do anything – they are the unity of heavenly and earthly powers.

At end of the same chapter there is a section about the decline of life:

'At 80 the *qi* of the lung declines and the *po* leave. This is why one has difficulty speaking.'

This is referring to the *qi* of the lung, not the *po* in their general meaning that we saw earlier in the same chapter. The text goes on to 90 and 100, so the person is not yet dead, but there is a decline with difficulty in speaking and breathing.

In the medical texts, when *hun* and *po* are presented together, they should be understood as the foundation of the life of the mind and of the soul. If they leave and scatter, this will affect behaviour, in a way which suggests madness. But, as we have seen, in the Neijing there is also a very specific use of *po*, referring to both the lung and the *yin*, the body and the fluids, and specifically to the *yin* and the substances. *Po men* (魄 門), the gate of the *po*, is the name for the anus, and *po* (魄) is in fact very similar to another character, also pronounced *po* (粕), and which means the stool. Here a grain of millet (米) is the radical of the character. The expression *po men* (魄 門) can also be used for the pores, but often the term *gui men* (鬼 門, gate of the *gui*) is used. It says in Suwen chapter 11 that the anus (*po men* 魄 門) is a distant servant for the five *zang*, by allowing the elimination of the turbid. There are many other possible names for both the anus and the pores.

In some texts the *po* are linked with the body fluids, as representing the vital substances. These fluids leave the body after death, and in the same way the flesh decomposes. So it is not only the blood, but also the body fluids which express the vital substance linked with the *po*. In Suwen chapter 14 there is a description of a disorder in the five *zang* that leads to an invasion of fluid, and there is a sentence which says that 'only the *po* remain':

> 'There are diseases which do not emerge from the finest body hair; instead the *yang* (*qi*) is exhausted in the five *zang*. The body fluids fill the defences. The *po* resides alone. The essence is weakened in the interior. The *qi* vanishes from the exterior. One cannot protect the body with clothing (the body is swollen).'

The text of Suwen chapter 14 does not refer to a mental condition, but to an invasion by *yin* fluids due to a weakness of the *qi*. *Po* is used here in context that has little to do with the concept of souls, but represents the *yin* of the body – an excess of liquids. If the *yang* of the five *zang* is exhausted, the root of *qi* is deficient, transportation and transformation cannot take place, pathological fluids accumulate in the abdomen, making circulation even more difficult and the deficiency of *qi* even more severe. Such a person is bloated, with oedema and fluid retention, unable to put on their clothes, which no longer fit.

Another expression for a symptom relating to the *po* is *po han* (魄 汗) – the sweat of the *po*, in which is a profuse pathological sweat. We find it, for instance, in Suwen chapters 3 and 7:

'If the sweat of the *po* flows unceasingly, the physical form (*xing* 形) is weakened and the *qi* melts away.' (Suwen chapter 3)

'If *yin* struggles inside, *yang* creates havoc on the outside. The sweat of the *po* is not retained and a fourfold countercurrent (*si ni* 四 逆) emerges in the limbs. When it comes out it steams the lung and the person pants loudly. (Suwen chapter 7)

The basic explanation is a weakness of *qi* related to the lung, which is also present in the layers of the skin and responsible for the good functioning of the pores, which is of course the defensive *qi* (*wei qi* 衛 氣). The *qi* is too weak to keep the fluids in their correct form and circulation, or to control the opening and closing of the pores. So fluids leave the body by the 'gates of the *po*', the pores of the skin.

But are the *po* leaving the body as well? Not exactly. They do not leave the body in the same way that they do after death, the person is still alive, and may remain alive for many years, but it is the sign of an imbalance which can lead to separation and death if it gets worse. And is this a pathology of the *po*? It is basically a weakness of the lung *qi*, but it results in a loss of what actually forms the body. And is there an effect on the mind? Possibly, as is the case with every kind of pathology.

A similar example with the *hun*, and a symptom called 'the *hun* are no longer kept in their dwelling place'. As we saw in Lingshu chapter 8, the dwelling place of the *hun* is the blood, and more specifically, the blood of the liver. When the liver is full of good quality blood, its physiological activity is balanced by the *yin* quality of the blood and its mental activity is inspired by the spiritual awareness pervading the blood. Sound projects, reasonable plans, firm decisions, and no emotional blockage are the result. But when the blood of the liver is deficient, excitement disturbs the reason, projects cannot be completed, the imagination uncontrolled. The *hun* are not housed as they ought to be.

As it is said in Suwen chapter 10, when one is at rest, asleep, the blood returns to the liver. Then the *hun* are empowered. They can visit the spirits. But this requires a harmonious balance between blood and *hun*. In the case of deficiency of blood, the *hun* may be over-excited, lacking root, unleashed. They may leave the body, but in an unordered way.

It is at night that the first symptoms of liver blood deficiency are felt, and it is in dreams that the symptoms are developed. Dreams are the activity of the *hun*, when consciousness is no longer within the intellect. But this activity is disturbed by the lack of blood in the liver. Instead of receiving inspiration and nourishment from the rich blood, the *hun* become excited and loose. Images in dreams are plethoric, exhausting the vitality during sleep.

A final example of the link between the *hun* and the liver and the *po* and the lung is found in the points bladder 42 and 47. Bladder 47, (*hun men* 魂 門) is located to the side of the back *shu* point of the liver (Bl 18); bladder 42 (*po hu* 魄 戶) to the side of the back *shu* point of the lung (Bl 13). When the characters *men* (門) and *hu* (戶) are used to speak of two different kinds of door, *men* is often used for a large door, opening to the exterior of the house; while *hu* is used for a small door, possibly between two rooms, within the interior. *Men* is a gate linked with the *yang*; *hu* is a door linked with the *yin* and associated with the earth. These two points work on the liver and the lung. Bladder 47 may also treat symptoms related to the heart/mind, palpitations, cardialgia, mental agitation and insomnia. Bladder 13 treats symptoms in the upper part of the back and linked to invasions due to lack of *qi*, such as cold, wind and heat.

Each time *hun* and *po* are mentioned in medical texts, it is very important to consider the context. The context is always clear within each text. This is particularly true with the *po*, which may in some contexts refer to a part of the soul and in other cases, to the pathological domination of the body by the *yin*.

So the *hun* and *po* may represent all the souls of a human being, both heavenly and earthly *qi*, the condition of their life, and their separation and departure at death. They encompass *yin yang*, body spirit, blood and *qi*. When seen as two of the five spirits, they represent the movement of *qi* proper to the elements wood and metal, and subsequently they may be used in certain contexts to represent this element or the *zang* related to it; liver or lung. In this instance, and only in this instance, *hun* and *po* may be put in a relationship with the other of the five aspects of spirit to represent the pattern of the five elements. These relationships make no sense otherwise.

58   ASPECTS OF SPIRIT

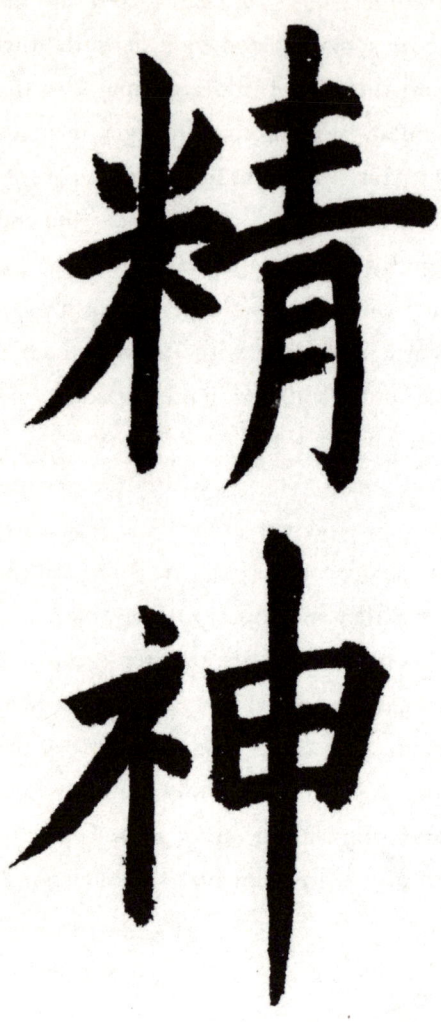

jing shen

JING SHEN

Spirits (*shen* 神) are seen in the most ancient texts as powers and deities, which are separate from and above human beings. The spirits were worshipped by human beings, and they were often linked to the spirits of the ancestors. But at a certain time in history, these spirits began to be associated with form (*xing* 形) and with the human body, and this evolved into a continuous interaction and interdependency between the body and the spirits. We will look at this evolution of the concept of spirits, how the spirits became associated with the heart, with stillness, and the source of wisdom to guide the activities of life.

Then we will return to the essences (*jing* 精) to see how they are linked both to cosmic life and also to the life of every creature, particularly human beings. In some texts we will find *jing* (精 essences) and *shen* (神 spirits) used in very similar ways, as if they are almost the same thing, but we can also find examples of the essences linked more closely to substance – but always with substance that is so refined it is almost formless. It is not possible to say that the essences have form and the spirits have no form, because the relationship between essences and form is very subtle; but spirit is always linked to a living being, and essences to the vitality necessary to implement life – either within what has form or in what is formless. Calm stillness is the very first condition for the essences to be pure and powerful and also for the spirits to be present.

Then we will come to *jing shen* (精 神, vital spirit), which is the association of essences and spirits as that which is most precious to human life. *Jing shen* is built every day, and constitutes the best of what we are able to be as human beings. We will also look at the *shen ming* (神 明), spiritual brightness, or radiance of the spirits, and see how they are related to the vital spirit (*jing shen* 精 神) – how they are seen both as an external reality and something within each being, which includes all the transformations which make life. The visible reality of life manifests the invisible presence of the spirits.

After that we will look at the medical texts to see how the same kind of expression is seen in medicine. The vital spirit is linked to health because it is the very basic condition for life and for the *qi* to function well. It allows each person to follow the evolution and transformation which makes up individual life; it governs interactions with surroundings, so that it is possible to live correctly, remain true to the innate nature, and make the best of life's potential. This is not only good health, but clarity of mind, which is vital for every practitioner in order to make a clear diagnosis and to give an accurate treatment.

Spirits and wind

Before the first appearance of the character *shen* (神) itself, there was a strong belief in the spirits of the ancestors as well as in the spirits as natural forces. The two concepts were very close and sometimes the same: a powerful ancestor might become a god attached to a natural phenomenon. In heaven, the ancestors submitted to the supreme deity, called the High Sovereign or emperor above (*shang di* 上 帝), who probably was also the first ancestor of the dynasty, or of the king's lineage).

One of the most important themes found on the ancient inscriptions (*jia gu wen* 甲 骨 文) is the combination of the idea of spirits and winds – more precisely, the four phoenix-winds, four spirits represented by phoenixes (*feng* 鳳) who sent influences to earth in the manner of the wind (*feng* 風). They were sent by the High Sovereign to the four territories which formed the earth, bringing life to each of them according to their natural position.

What appears nowadays as a metaphor was then most probably believed to be a reality: the wind brings life from heaven to earth; it penetrates the earth through its openings, which were seen as caverns in the mountains (*feng xue* 風穴), which are also where the phoenixes settled at sunset. Blowing in the spring, the phoenix winds triggered the process of transformation, leading to germination, growth of vegetation, and the maturation of crops.

There was not only one wind, but several, traditionally called the eight winds, corresponding to the directions of the compass. Each wind brings life to each space on earth, according to its own specificities, and determined by its position. The wind is both one and multiple, as is the spirit (*shen* 神) or the *qi* (氣). It is one because it comes from one source and shares the same nature and features; multiple because, when it is expressed on earth, it is always specific: the north wind and the east wind are different, one may bring rain another drought.

Wind and spirit (and later *qi*) share the same basic qualities: they bring life from heaven to earth, they start the process of transformation, leading life to take form according to its innate quality. They allow the manifestation on earth of what is above.

As it is said in the Shuowen Jiezi :

'The spirits are the spirits of heaven (*tian shen* 天神) which cause all beings to appear.'

The character shen (神)

Ancient forms of the character *shen* (示申) can be found on bronzes of the Western Zhou (1046-770 BCE), where it has the meaning of the spirits of the ancestors. The ancestors are in heaven in the company of the supreme deity, or the supreme ancestor, literally the emperor above Shang di (上 帝).

The later character *shen* (神) has two parts. The left part of the character (示), is also very old. The image is of something descending – and the character is found in oracular inscriptions where it indicates a descent from heaven to earth, a manifestation from above. It appears in the Jiaguwen, the earliest Chinese writing, with the meaning of the place where the spirits manifest themselves during a sacrifice – possibly an altar for ancestral worship. But as early as the Eastern Zhou dynasty (770-221 BCE), the character has the meaning of manifestation, especially of a manifestation from heaven, such as an omen, a portent or a warning, as well as the manifestation of the ancestors through ritual. This part of the character (示) took on the meaning of something becoming perceptible, and it gradually came to mean to manifest, to show, to give a sign or even a teaching, or to make someone alert to something. Later, it simply has the meaning to show, to become manifest or known.

The right part is the phonetic (申), and has been used since ancient times to indicate a date or a period of time; it is the name of the ninth of the twelve earthly branches. The ninth earthly branch corresponds to the seventh month of the year, the limit of expansion and extension and hence the beginning of the *yin*, the beginning of autumn and the decline of the sun. This is the time when everything – in both nature and human beings – naturally moves from stretching and extension (the expansion of the *yang*) into the contraction of the *yin*. In commentaries written some

1000 years later, it is said to mean to stretch and expand. If you add the character for a human being (*ren* 人) the character (*shen* 伸) means to stretch and extend; with the character for silk (紳) it means a long belt with hanging ties.

The completed character *shen* (神), which appears later, has the meaning of what we may call spirits; it encompasses the spirits of the ancestors, but more generally refers to all beneficial influences coming from above and manifesting on earth. *Shen* (神) always implies a superior or divine power, exerting influence and affecting nature and human beings. Because it is subtle, it is also mysterious and imperceptible. We can see the effect of the presence of the spirits, but we cannot see the spirits themselves. We can see the fertility of the land, and perhaps this is because of offerings made to the deity of the spring. The same character *shen* can therefore have the meaning of something marvellous, prodigious, supernatural – something that we cannot understand. We cannot see the spirits act, but we can see their effect. But they can also manifest as a sign of disorder – particularly in human behaviour. Disorderly human behaviour will cause disorder in nature, and if our behaviour is disorderly, the ancestors will send signs to tell us to change.

The character jing 精

This character is also made in two parts; one is a seed or grain of cereal bursting open (米), and the other is the colour green (青), or more specifically, the colour of life – it is the external manifestation of the quality of the life-force – that which is within made visible to the eye.

The earliest meaning of this character *jing* (精) is that of the very best quality of grains, which made the best possible flour. It is the most pure, refined flour, without any husk or impurities, and it also has the meaning of being the best, the elite, the first choice of something. It is fine and delicate, and not only has a good taste, but is also full of nourishment. *Jing* (精) has all of these meanings: to be refined, exquisite, excellent and very subtle – and at the same time it is something that by its richness and purity is able to give life and to make life function well. It is the substrate of life; the vitality. The essences are sometimes considered to be a concentration of *qi*, that is, *qi* led by a *yin* movement. This concentrated state of *qi* is the vital substance which allows a life to take form.

Essences are the basis of life. We must eat in order to remain alive, and the essences are what enable us to continue life within the body – not simply to survive, but to be full of strength. When we stop eating our mental and physical strength declines; the essences of food are at the very basis of physical life. These essences provide the *yin*, the form of the body, and they give the condition for any life to develop and to continue its development on earth, because they also enable the renewal of *qi*, and are the support of the *yang*. *Jing* (精) is the very basis of matter for any living being, and the purer they are the better.

JING SHEN IN CLASSICAL TEXTS

It will become clear as we look at the texts, that it is impossible to reach a precise definition that can be applied to all texts. Even if we limit ourselves to classical texts before the common era, we will find that the meaning varies according to the context. But although it is impossible to apply a fixed meaning to the terms *jing shen* (精 神) and *shen ming* (神 明), there is a consistent vision, though it may be expressed by using these characters in what may appear to be conflicting ways. Sometimes, for example, essences may be used with a meaning close to that of spirits; the radiance of the spirits, or spiritual brightness (*shen ming* 神明) may have the same meaning as the spirits (*shen* 神). All this is possible within the early classical texts.

As we have seen with the *hun* and the *po*, the vision of *jing* and *shen* is not always the same in classical philosophical and classical medical texts; the meaning of the terms *shen* (神), *jing* (精), *shen ming* (神明), *jing ming* (精明) may change according to context. We will see that there is an evolving vision of the notion of the vital spirit and of its reality within a human being, and that this is an important basis, not only for the more philosophical understanding of what it means to be human, but also in medicine. The concept of *jing shen* is at the very basis of medicine, even though within the medical texts the more philosophical aspects of these ideas are not discussed. The expression *jing shen* actually appears in no more than twelve chapters of the Neijing, both Suwen and Lingshu, but nevertheless, the meaning is implied and understood.

First, we will look at this vision in the non-medical texts from the 5th to the 1st centuries BCE, and then we will look at a selection of medical texts. In some texts the expressions are used in the same way as in the earlier philosophical texts, but there is also a special way in which they are understood within medical literature. This is especially so when the *shen* are presented as a series of five, the so called five aspects of the spirit (*wu shen* 五神), which are usually related to the five elements and the five *zang* organs. In this case, as we have seen with *hun* and *po*, they may represent an aspect of the function of the associated organ, and this is a completely different level of understanding.

Chunqiu Zuozhuan

This is a text from the 5th - 4th centuries BCE, and we only have a few classical texts written by scholars from that time: there were many beliefs and stories that are not recorded. Certainly if we were to speak with the ordinary people of China some 2,500 years ago, there would be many stories of spirits and deities, temples, altars, ghosts and spirits of the ancestors returning and manifesting themselves here and there. These texts provide some examples of this early thinking, before we move on to the vision of the spirits within human beings.

Duke Zhuang, year 32:

'In Autumn in the seventh month there was the descent of a spirit in Xing. King Hui asked Guo, the historiographer of the interior, the reason for it. He replied: When a state is about to flourish, intelligent spirits (*shen ming* 神 明) descend to survey its virtue. When it is going to perish, spirits also descend to behold the wickedness. Thus there have been instances of states flourishing from spirits appearing and also of states perishing. Cases in point may be adduced from the dynasty of Yu, Shao, Shang and Jou.

'The king then asked: What should be done in the case of this spirit? Guo replied: Present it with its own offerings, which are those proper to the day on which it came. (The manifestation is always linked to the time.) The king acted accordingly and the historiographer went to the state of Guo and presented the offerings. There he heard that the Duke of the State of Guo had been requesting the favour of enlarged territory from the spirit, and on his return he said: The

State of Guo is sure to perish. The Duke is oppressive and listens to spirits. The spirit stayed for six months. When the Duke asked the prayer master Yin, the superintendent of the ancestral temple Chu, and the historiographer to sacrifice to it, the spirit promised to give him territory. The historiographer said, Ha! The State of Guo will perish, I have heard that when a State is about the flourish, its ruler receives its lessons from the people, and when it is about to perish it receives its lessons from spirits. The spirits are intelligent, correct and impartial, their course is regulated by the conduct (*xing* 行) of men. The slenderness of the State of Guo's virtue extends to many things, how can any increase of territory be obtained.'

We can see that in this text there is not much difference between *shen* and *shen ming*. The spirit manifests itself in a visible form, in this case some kind of unusual bird, which has come to the temple. If this is a spirit, it is important to make offerings, which must be appropriate to the day when the spirit appeared. Spirits may appear when a state is flourishing, because they are attracted by virtue, but they may also come to give a sign that the state is not in a good condition. The ruler did not understand this; he thought that the spirits had come to grant him a favour and he asked for the increase of his territory. Guo explained that the increase of territory can only come from correct behaviour, and is not something that can be given by the spirits.

Several things are mixed together here: there are all kinds of popular beliefs about the spirits and offering sacrifices in order to obtain what we want to receive. We give the spirits what we think they want, and in return we ask for something for ourselves. But in this text we can see that there is already the understanding that this is not the right way to behave. It does not happen like that. You will increase your territory, and achieve whatever you want to achieve, only by your behaviour. Good fortune will come if you are full of virtue and behave correctly – not because you have made a sacrifice to the spirits. The text does not deny the reality of spirits, but it denies the fact that you can make some kind of bargain with them; you cannot behave as you like and then make a bargain with the spirits – it doesn't work like that. On the other hand, that does not mean that the spirits do not exist. It is not possible to make a request of a spirit of heaven for something that is not part of the natural order of the cosmos. To do so is to be in a state of delusion, and to bring calamity on oneself and the kingdom.

Duke Huan Year 6:
'To rule according to the way (*dao* 道) is to show a loyal love for the people and a faithful worship of the spirits (*shen* 神). The condition of the people is what the spirits look for; the sage kings therefore secured the welfare of the people, and then put their strength into serving the spirits.'

To take care of the people, as a good faithful ruler, is to worship the spirits. It is the condition of the people that the spirits consider to be important. It is important to serve the spirits, but not instead of serving the people. At the level of the individual, one must take care of oneself and one's family first, and then worship the spirits. One must not do one instead of the other. Again, this would be a misunderstanding of the meaning of heaven and the heavenly, or natural, development of any situation.

Duke Xi Year 10:
'The ruler of Qin had the body of the late heir Prince Gong moved to a new grave. In the autumn, Hu Tu, Prince Tsun Sheng's former carriage driver was on his way to one of the lesser towns when he encountered the late prince.'

We may be surprised that the prince went to meet his carriage driver, but we have to remember that the carriage driver and the owner of the carriage had a very close relationship at that time. They travelled together, hunted together, fought together in war, and so they relied on one another for their lives. It is the same in other civilizations at that time, for example in India, where in the Mahabharata Krishna is the charioteer to Prince Arjuna. It was certainly not a lowly position and their relationship was very close.

'The prince ordered him to climb up into his own carriage and had him act as charioteer.'

So is this a ghost carriage? Are we in some kind of other world?

'The Prince announced to Hu Tu, My father has no concern for ritual. I have asked the Emperor of Heaven to punish him, heaven will hand the state of Jin over to Qin. Qin will carry on the sacrifice to me.'

This is a common theme in stories of this time. The spirit of a dead man is not happy with something that has happened on earth. Here it is a problem with ritual, and he has referred it to the Emperor of Heaven, who has the power to bring good and bad fortune, asking him to intervene. Here again there is the idea of a superior power with the ability to interfere with human destiny.

> 'Hu Tu replied: I have heard that the spirits do not accept sacrifice from those who are not of their own kind. And the people do not offer sacrifice to those who are not of their own clan. If the ruling house of Qin is destroyed, then how can the sacrifice made to you not fail to be cut off? Moreover, what fault have the people of Qin committed? You propose to inflict punishment on people who do not deserve it, and to wipe out your own sacrifice. I think you had better reconsider the matter.'

So what are the spirits here? And could it possibly be a good thing to be unfair towards so many people just to have personal revenge? This behaviour will also cut him off from the sacrifice.

> 'The Prince says: I will ask the Emperor once more. Seven days from now there will be a shaman in the western outskirts of the new city, you can meet with me there through him.'

So here we have the manifestation of spirits through a shaman.

> 'Hu Tu agreed to this and the Prince disappeared. When the time came and Hu Tu went to the designated place, the Prince announced: The Emperor has given me permission to punish the guilty party, he will meet defeat at Han.'

This text is a good example of a very common understanding of *shen* in China, not only in the 5th century BCE, but over a very long period of time. This text is interesting because it shows this common understanding of the spirits, but also Hu Tu's reflection on this. Do the spirits really control our destiny, or do we control our destiny through our behaviour, as part of the natural order, with the spirits simply being the manifestation of that?

In the philosophical texts we can see that this kind of reflection continues, and becomes the common vision of life, a life which is not ruled by external powers. The spirits, even the spirits of heaven, do not control our destiny, they rule the transformation of cosmic life, and that is nothing other than the natural order. Human beings are responsible, through their behaviour, for what happens to them. That is not to say that the spirits don't exist, but that they are nothing other than the heavenly laws or natural order.

Lunyu, Analects of Confucius (551-479)

In the text of the Lunyu, we see that Confucius refers to the spirits, and suggests that these spirits deserve some kind of worship. But Confucius speaks about the necessity of personal involvement when worshipping the spirits. In chapter 3 line 12 the master says:

'If I myself do not participate in the sacrifice, it is as though I have not sacrificed at all.'

And in chapter 8 line 21:

'As for the Sage-king Yu, I find no fault with him at all. He was simple in his food and drink and yet was generous in his devotion to the gods and spirits of his ancestors.'

There is a very famous story when Confucius was seriously ill, and one of his disciples asked if he may pray on his behalf. The master said:

'It is done. …I have already been praying for myself for a long time now.'

There are several interpretations of the meaning of this text, but the important thing for us is that within the Lunyu – which is one of the most important books of Chinese civilization, and one of the foundations of the way of thinking – the spirits are a part of that reality; the spirits of the ancestors, but even more, the spirits of heaven and earth. There are nevertheless, powers that we should keep at a distance. For instance, chapter 6 line 22:

'Fan Chi asked about wisdom (*zhi* 知 – perfect consciousness). The master said: To undertake the duty assigned to the people, respect ghosts and spirits (*gui shen* 鬼 神) but keep them at a distance. This may be said to be wisdom.'

The idea of keeping them at a distance is similar to what we found in the Chunqiu Zuozhuan; it is not good to court them and ask for personal favours. You can respect them but not attempt to use them. This is a very famous quotation from the Lunyu, which says that the master did not talk about spirits. There are things that we do not speak about, and he did not speak about strange happenings or disorder in nature and spirits.

In book 11 line 12, a disciple asks how to serve the spirits and gods (*gui shen* 鬼 神, the spirits of heaven and earth). The master replies:

'Not yet being able to serve other people, how will you be able to serve the spirits?'

The instruction is first to do your duty and serve the people, and after that you will know how to serve the spirits – because it is no different. Then he asked about death, and the master replied:

'Not yet understanding life, how can you understand death?'

Confucius was not eluding the question, but putting things in the right perspective. It is not to say that the spirits are a secondary thing, but first you need to be a perfect human being, and then you will automatically serve the spirits, including the spirits of the ancestors. If you understand what life is, then you will put death in its rightful place. There is no point trying to do the reverse, it does not work.

Xunzi: Change and transformation

In the text of Xunzi, a Confucian philosopher from the first half of the 3rd century BCE, the spirits are seen as cosmic power linked to vital transformation:

'To bring completion without acting, to obtain without seeking – this is the work of heaven. Thus, although the sage has deep understanding, he does not attempt to exercise it upon the work of heaven. Though he has great talents, he does not attempt to apply it to the work of heaven.'

The sage will not try to make crops grow faster than normal, or to make the wind and rain come when he wants them to. He does not imagine that anything he might do would be better than that which happens naturally – or according to heaven. It is always important to remember that within these texts heaven is not a place but a power directing life.

'He has keen perception, but does not attempt to use it on the work of heaven, hence it is said that he does not compete with heaven's work. Heaven has its seasons, earth has its richness, human beings have their government.'

Heaven has its seasons, which are the unfolding of the natural order. Earth has the richness of all that is produced, human beings have the ability to govern, to rule, to administer, (*zhi* 治, which may also be translated as to treat and to cure). This is one of the key words for human beings – to rule and govern, both at the level of the state, but also to treat, govern and organize oneself. In the Xunzi, the idea of the three powers (*san cai* 三才), heaven, earth and human beings, is already developed, and this ability or power to rule and govern is commonly associated with human beings. It refers to the ability to follow the natural order and integrate it into one's life, by observation of the work of heaven and its reaction on earth. To indulge one's desires, rather than follow the natural order, is to create disorder.

'…All things receive what is nourishing for them and work towards their completion. One does not see the process taking place, but sees only the result. And that is called the spirits (*shen* 神).'

In this text, the spirits are the result of the great transformations of the *yin yang* – one does not see the process taking place but sees only the result. Everything is in harmony. So here there is a link between the notion of the spirits and the notion of harmony. Spirits are like harmony – and if there is no harmony, then there is death.

> 'All men understand the formless forces that bring things about, hence it is called the accomplishment of heaven. Only the sage does not seek to understand heaven.'

With our limited knowledge we cannot understand the very mechanisms of life. We can understand and see all the transformations of the *yin yang*, and we can analyse that, but what is behind this transformation, what brings it into being, is the work of heaven, and that is out of the reach of the understanding possible within our limited body, limited brain, limited sense organs, limited knowledge and limited perception. But we may be able to recognize the result of this process as the accomplishment of heaven, which is the spirits.

This is very close to ideas expressed in the Xici, the Great Commentary to the Book of Change, which was written at about the same time:

> 'What cannot be probed by the *yin yang* is called spirits.'

And also from the Xici:

> 'Understanding the way of change and transformation is how one perceives the spirits.'

This is the same vision – we cannot know the spirits, but can know all the various forms of change and transformation which occur in the universe, which are the manifestation of the spirits. This is not so distant from the idea of the manifestation of the spirits as ancestors, or as benevolent powers which help the state to flourish, or bring strange signs of disorder. There is always some kind of manifestation, but in these later texts it is a more cosmic view. Here it is the work of heaven, and the development of the natural order is seen as a kind of self-perpetuating and self-regulating process. Coming back to the text of Xunzi chapter 17:

> 'When the work of heaven is established and its accomplishments brought to completion, when the form of man is whole and his spirits are present, then love and hate, delight and anger, sorrow and joy find lodging in him.'

The spirits are seen here as that which enable the cosmic metamorphosis, the work of heaven or the natural order, and following that, the same spirits are seen as inhabiting a human body, and allowing the perception of feelings and emotions which are both the best and the worst of human life. When the spirits are present, feelings and emotions come at the appropriate time, there is no excess, and they do not last longer than is natural. The form has to be complete for the spirits to appear, as we see during the development of the foetus in pregnancy (cf: Pregnancy and Gestation, Monkey Press 2007). It is during the 10th month of pregnancy that the body form is complete and the spirits also are complete.

> 'This is called natural disposition (*tian qing* 天情). The ears, eyes, nose, mouth and body enable us to perceive, but they cannot be substituted one for another. They are called the heavenly faculties. The heart dwells in the centre and governs through the five senses.

Hence it is called the heavenly master (*tian zhu* 天 主).'

The heart is the lord and sovereign, responsible for heaven or the natural order and therefore the unfolding of life in a harmonious way within us. This is accomplished by the spirits. If the spirits are complete, the heart is able to be the heavenly master, and everything is done according to the natural order.

Huainanzi

This same idea appears in the Huainanzi, which is a later text, from around 150 - 130 BCE. In chapter 1 we see that the two powers of ancient times, the two heavenly deities or spirits, possibly Fuxi and Nugua, took hold of the handles of the *dao* and stood at its centre. With the spirits, they roamed together in transformation, to bring peace and order in the four directions. This, of course, is a metaphor – but it implies that if the *dao* is the way things proceed, and that which allows things to proceed by themselves, it may be expressed by the idea of spirits or deities in a central position, extending their transformation in the four directions bringing natural organization, which is life.

'The spirits reside in the tiniest tip of autumn down and yet are larger than the sum total of the cosmos.'

The spirits through their transformation are everywhere. They are in the tiniest hair, and at the same time larger than the cosmos. So when we speak of the spirits as this power of transformation, it is everywhere, from the smallest possible thing to the largest.

Xici

At the beginning of the second part of the Xici we see:

'When Baxi reigned over all under heaven, he looked up and saw the symbols in heaven, he looked down and saw the patterns on earth. Close at hand he made inferences for his own person; far away he made inferences for other things, hence he created the eight trigrams to penetrate the virtue of spiritual illumination (*shen ming* 神明) and to classify the natures of the myriad things.'

The change and transformation of the cosmos, which is a way to know the spirits, allows us to look at the manifestation in heaven and earth and by inference we may have an idea of the natural order and the process of the development of life. From observing these changes we can penetrate the virtue of the *shen ming* (神明) – the complete manifestation of the spirits. We can do that through understanding the trigrams, but also by using the yarrow stalks for divination of the Yijing. The name given to the yarrow stalks in the Xici is *shen wu* (神物), spiritual things.

When the yarrow stalks are counted it is important to remember that numbers represent the natural law. By the use of numbers, we are able to penetrate the manifestation of the spirits, through the transformation of the cosmos, and thus find our place in this order.

Zhuangzi

Generally speaking, by around 100 BCE, the spirits were considered as that which is formless (*wu xing* 無形), the body as that which has form *xing* (形). But as we already saw in the Xunzi chapter 17, there is a correlation between the completion of the body and the appearance or presence of the spirits within the body form. The same idea is expressed in the Zhuangzi Chapter 12:

'In the great beginning there was non-being (*wu* 無), there was no being, no name. Out of it arose the One (*yi* 一).'

Non-being is nothing; that which is not a being. This is also a way to speak of unity. Manifestation implies separation, so unity implies not yet existing. Non-being contains the potential for making all beings and things, but no beings or things are yet manifest. To call that the One, is to see it as the potential for all the other numbers, and therefore as the potentiality of the development of the differentiation of the two, and the emergence of *qi*, which is the three. As we find in Laozi chapter 42:

'The *dao* generates the one, the one generates the two, the two generates the three, the three generates the ten thousand things.'

There is not really a difference between that which exists but is not yet formed as a being, and the One. But if we want to speak of the great beginning, we have to speak of the Oneness, which is the infinite depths of reality:

'There was One, but it had no form. Things or beings (*wu* 物) got hold of it and came to life, and it was called virtue (*de* 德, the efficient manifestation of the *dao*, the vital power). Before things had form, they had their allotted nature, these were of many kinds, but not cut off from one another. And they were called destiny (*ming* 命).'

Each being with a form has its own determination and qualities and therefore its own allotted nature and destiny. Each being has its own way to accomplish its life by being completely faithful to its true nature. Each being has its own place and its own way to evolve in life. This is called *ming* (命), which we translate as fate or destiny.

> 'Out of the flow and flux, things were born, and as they grew, they developed distinctive shapes, these were called forms (*xing* 形).'

This character *xing* (形) suggests an organization specific to a species.

> 'The forms and bodies held within them spirits, each with its own characteristics and limitations, and this was called the natural endowment (*tian qing* 天情).'

This is another example of the relationship between the completion of the body form, with its distinctive shapes and features, and the ability of the spirits to be present. There are spirits everywhere, in the tiniest autumn down, as well as in the widest reaches of the cosmos, but at the same time, if we look at each living being, with its own specific features, a name, a shape and a body, we may speak of spirits within the body form. There must first be a body form. If there is no form to welcome the spirits and offer them a place to rest, they cannot be present. But because the body form has specific features, it also has limitations. A human being follows all the fluctuations of life, but must always remain true to the inborn nature, or natural endowment, *tian qing* (天情). I can transform my own body in order to become as a heavenly spirit, and if I follow my inborn nature, I will be part of the cosmic metamorphosis as a whole.

In Zhuangzi chapter 24, there is the story of a sage who visits a prince, and says: 'I want to bring comfort to your spirits and body (*shen xing* 神形)'. The prince asks what he means and after reminding the prince of his position and responsibilities the sage says:

> 'The spirits love harmony (*he* 和) and hate licentiousness; licentiousness is a sickness and that is why I have come to offer my comfort.'

In order to rule our lives, the most important thing is harmony. If we do not have harmony, we cannot live, and to have harmony implies to have no excess. This is seen very clearly with the emotions, but also in the way that we treat our physical body – and the appetites and desires which begin in the body. Spiritual brightness (*shen ming* 神明), the intelligence, or self-knowledge brought about by the presence of the spirits, is needed in order to control the body and the senses, which have the power to destroy the harmony of life and the integration of individual life with the universe. The spirits hate licentiousness, they hate the lack of harmony! And the spirits are within us, so why do we indulge in licentiousness?

Here in Zhuangzi chapter 24, the sage does not say, 'I want to bring comfort to your spirits', he says I want to bring comfort to your spirits and body! Because if the body is damaged, the spirits are unable to express themselves fully. When the body is complete, the spirits are able to be complete, as we saw in Xunzi chapter 17:

> 'When the body is complete, then the spirits appear.'

The Historical Records of Sima Qian

We see this again in the Shiji, the Historical Records of Sima Qian, chapter 130:

> 'Thus, what makes life in a human being? It is the spirits. And what is able to receive them? It is the body. When one makes too great a use of the spirits, they are exhausted, and when one makes too great use of the body, the body is also exhausted.'

This suggests that it is possible to over-use and exhaust the spirits, as well as the body. In both cases the result is exhaustion and even death, caused by the separation of body and spirit. The text does not refer to one of the five spirits that are specific to the medical texts, but to the forces which enable vital transformation – and which exist within a human being in the power of the mind, the intelligence, and a brightness, clarity and accuracy of the intellect. If they are not present within the body, there will be death. We cannot survive this separation. Once one is dead there is no way to come back to life. The separation of body and spirits is final. The sages' vision of life was based on this understanding. The spirits are the source and foundation of life, and the body its implementation.

> 'The one who wants to govern all under heaven without having first stabilized the spirits – how could that be possible?'

This is the same as in Zhuangzi chapter 24; it is through the cultivation of the spirits within the body that we are able to rule, either our own selves or the kingdom. In the Historical Records chapter 25 it says:

'The spirits appear from what has no form, and then the form (*xing* 形, the body) is completed and has features and specificities. So it is said that the spirits activate the *qi*, and the *qi* determines the form. This body form has an inner organization which sustains its formation and continuation, and this inner organization determines each species and allows their classification.

'…Beings receive the spirits, but without understanding. They come and go, and that is the reason why the sage is fearful and desires to have the spirits present within him. His only desire is to keep their presence. He desires their presence in that way because nothing is more precious.'

The spirits come to the body, they master the *qi* which determine the body and all the body's functions. The spirits activate the *qi*, as we see also in Suwen chapter 14:

'…the spirits are not activating.'

The spirits are not sending any messages or commands, and that is the reason why the patient cannot react to the treatment, and declines. If the spirits are not activating the *qi*, there is no circulation or movement in the body, and the treatment therefore has no effect.

The body is not only a shape – but has its own principles of organization. Chinese medicine works on this inner organization of the living body and its system of classification. For all that to function well, the spirits must be activating all this. Our inborn nature as a human being gives us the potential for the presence of the spirits and we need to accept the brightness of the spirits (*shen ming* 神 明) so that they may manifest themselves. Within a human being this implies intelligence and understanding, which includes the way in which we conduct our lives. If we have this intelligence, we are illuminated enough to desire only the spirits. That makes us more and more eager to desire only the spirits. Illumination always has this kind of double effect; little by little, it rules the body, the sense organs, the desires, and then there will be no licentiousness.

The body alone is not enough for life. In Zhuangzi chapter 19 we can see the limitation of nourishing the body: we need to nourish the body and to keep it in a good state, but that should not be our main focus.

'He who has mastered the true nature (*qing* 性) of life (*sheng* 生) does not labour over what life cannot do. He who has mastered the true nature of fate (*ming* 命) does not labour over what knowledge cannot change. He who wants to nourish his body (*xing* 形) must first of all turn to things. And yet it is possible to have more than enough things and for the body still to go un-nourished. He who has life must first of all make sure that it does not leave the body.'

As we saw in Shiji chapter 130, the unity of the body and the spirits gradually becomes the definition of human life.

'And yet it is possible for life never to leave the body and still fail to be preserved.'

I may be a living being but I may not accept the radiance of the spirits nor allow them to manifest within me. I would therefore not build my life in and through my own spirits.

'The coming of life cannot be fended off, its departure cannot be stopped. How pitiful those who think that simply nourishing the body is enough to preserve life! But if nourishing the body is in the end not enough to preserve life, then why is what the world does worth doing? It may not be worth doing, and yet it cannot be left undone. This is unavoidable.'

There are things that we cannot avoid doing – even if I do not focus on nourishing the body, even if I say that nourishing the body is not enough to remain in the movement of life, yet there are things that I cannot avoid, like drinking water. The idea is to live life without too many entanglements, which exhaust the body, and avoid everything that injures the body. If you 'forget life', by being more in the movement of life than by trying to keep hold of life, then your vitality will be unimpaired.

'One who's body and vitality (*xing jing* 形 精) do not decline, is able to move. The vitality more and more refined (*jing er you jing* 精 而 又 精) one returns to become a helper of heaven (*xiang tian* 相 天).'

The perfect human being can move – from one situation to another, even from one form to another – following change and transformation. With body and mind increasingly pure and calm, such a being finally merges with the creative power of heaven. Vitality here is the essences (*jing* 精), and it is the essences, not the spirits, which are preserved. But essences and spirits are almost the same thing in this context. In other texts, such as the Huainanzi, the same thing is accomplished by the *jing shen*, (精 神) vital spirit. There is no real difference in meaning here between essences (*jing* 精), spirits (*shen* 神) and essences/spirits (*jing shen* 精 神). My vitality is what I do with my life and what makes my life.

At this time the spirits (*shen* 神) are still linked with heaven. For example in Zhuangzi chapter 13:

'Nothing so full of spirits as heaven, nothing so rich as earth, nothing so great as the emperor and king.'

Again we have here the three powers (*san cai* 三才) of heaven, earth and man – man represented here as the ruler. There is the richness of earth, and for heaven, spirits. In other texts we find that heaven has the four seasons and the natural order. In fact the spirits are what becomes manifest through all this work and life of the cosmos.

Guanzi chapter 49: Neiye

'The life of all human beings is as follows: heaven produces their essences, earth produces their form. The two unite to become a human being.'

We see in the Neiye that it is through the essences, or vitality (*jing* 精) that we are able to have the presence of the spirits. By concentrating the essences, maintaining a good quality of *qi*, which is also part of our vital forces, and by managing the activity of the *qi* in a good way (by following the four seasons, etc.) we may allow the spirits to be present within us. This means that we become more and more aligned with their heavenly nature, which is reflected in the clarity of mind and intelligence.

We have already seen that it is the spirits that activate the *qi*, and now, in the Neiye, we see that by concentrating the *qi*, the spirits can be present. Little by little, by turning within, back to my inborn nature,

I develop a feeling of what is good and bad for me. If I behave in such a way that my body is ruled by my consciousness, I will have more and more ability to receive the spirits and the brightness of the spirits. I will continue to concentrate my *qi*, clarify my essences and rectify my heart. This same idea is found everywhere.

> 'If you concentrate your *qi* until you become spirit-like, your grasp of all things will be complete. Can you concentrate? Can you focus?'

So the spirits in heaven are also within us; they are the power of awareness which allows us to have a human mind, to have perception. They allow knowledge and reaction, they allow us to be human – with the human capacity of knowledge and consciousness.

Huainanzi chapter 1

> 'Human beings are born tranquil (*jing* 靜). This is their inborn nature (heavenly nature, *tian zhi xing* 天 之 性). They move when roused, this is the stirring of the inborn nature. Things happen and the spirits respond.'

There is a response, for example within the breast of the mother; there are emotions and feelings. We respond because we have spirits, which enable both perception and response, and also the choice of whether to respond or not.

> 'This is the movement of consciousness (knowing, *zhi* 知). When consciousness comes into contact with things, feelings of attraction

and aversion are produced.'

We can take or reject, love or hate.

> 'When these feelings of attraction and aversion have form, and consciousness is seduced to the outside, one is unable to return to oneself, and the heavenly principles (the natural organization or underlying patterns, *tian li* 天理) are destroyed.'

The spirits here are the basis of consciousness – which includes feelings and emotions. This consciousness may or may not act to benefit the evolution of life; it can return to quiet tranquillity, or create disorder. By creating disorder, it goes against the nature of life and the principles of organization which manifest themselves within the body. The spirits do not have principles, they are principles. They are the way to do things, that which gives us the capacity to react, to be conscious. But either for the best or the worst.

Huainanzi chapter 7

> 'The body wears out but the spirits are not subject to transformation. It is because they are not transformed that they resonate with all transformations. A thousand changes and ten thousand twists and turns, and not even the beginning of its limits. That which is transformed returns and reverts to the formless. That which is not transformed shares the same life with heaven and earth.'

Here the difference between the body and the spirits is stated very clearly. The spirits are not transformed, they are the transformers. The body may wear out – but the spirits are the power of awareness and the total functioning of consciousness. If the spirits are of heaven, and operating as a part of cosmic life, they cannot be worn out. The spirits are simply the natural way of life, the heavenly laws and principles acting behind everything. But human beings do not allow the spirits to be as they are. The spirits are only able to express themselves through what I am.

In Huainanzi 7, the body wears out. In Zhuangzi we saw that the body can be worn out, but that it is also possible to wear out the spirits. But it is not quite the same. Here, the spirits are the cosmic spirits, and we have to become spirit-like. When it is a question of becoming spirit-like, for example by the concentration of *qi*, it is to become like the spirits of heaven. But as human beings we express the spirits through a body, which is unavoidable, and through the body we indulge all our desires. So the body can go against the harmony of the movement of life, which is necessary for the spirits to express what they are. But human beings also have the ability to develop a heart/mind (*xin* 心), which is not exactly a reflection of the spirits of heaven, but which is nevertheless an expression of the spirits, in the capacity to think, to be aware, to have consciousness; to react and therefore to know.

Therefore the question is always the same – how can we act in such a way so that little by little the mind becomes illuminated and the desire is only for more of this brightness emanating from the spirits? The answer is to always keep the purity of the vitality, and the richness and clarity of the essences by maintaining earthly life well and by allowing an opening to heavenly *qi*. In this text, it is the *jing shen*, the vital spirit, essences and spirits. When we are able to return to what is inborn, what is natural, we come back to a calmer, quiescent state: this means coming back to a more natural order of life, in which the light and brightness of the spirits can increase. In this case heart, knowledge and consciousness become the source of wisdom.

Huainanzi chapter 2

'Man is quiescent by nature, but covetousness and desires disturb him...'

All living beings have desires which pass through the sense organs, desires of sight, sound, taste, etc. and all the necessities of life pass through them too. The question in the text is:

'How is it that some attain spiritual brightness (*shen ming* 神明), while others cannot escape stupidity? It is because they are ruled differently. The spirits are the source of wisdom, when the source is clear, wisdom is bright (*ming* 明); wisdom is the sanctuary (*fu* 府) of the heart; when wisdom is universal, the heart is at peace, and when the heart is at peace it will rule everything correctly.'

Spirits and qi

There are many associations between spirits and *qi*. For example, in Huainanzi chapter 6:

'The mutual response (*gan ying* 感應) of things belonging to the same category is darkly mysterious and extremely subtle. Knowledge cannot explain it nor discussion unravel it. Thus when the external wind arrives, clear wine overflows; when the silk worm exudes its fresh silk, the string of the *shang* note snaps. Something has stirred them. When a drawing of the moon is traced in ashes, the moon's halo becomes incomplete. When a whale dies, comets appear. Something has activated them. Therefore when the sage rules, he treasures the way (*dao* 道) and does not speak, yet his kindness reaches the ten thousand people. But when ruler and minister distrust each other in their heart, concave and convex haloes appear in the sky. This is indeed evidence of the mutual influence of the *shen qi* (神氣).' (Based on the translation by Charles le Blanc)

What is called *shen qi* (神氣), spiritual *qi*, may also have other interpretations. For example, here it is understood as a naturalistic concept – the way in which the *qi* act under the influence of the spirits and thus correlate everything. At the time of the Huainanzi, the idea of correlation was well developed. Everything exists in the world through mutual correlation and correspondence. *Shen qi* is the way in which *qi* is organized according to this mutual resonance, and that happens because the spirits activate the *qi* – not only in the body but also in the cosmos. So *shen qi* may also be seen as a kind of supernatural emanation, a strange phenomenon, an emergence of *qi*, creating an effect of rainbow colours, which is seen as a sign of something abnormal.

In Zhuangzi chapter 21 *shen qi* is taken at the human level, where it has more connection with awareness and consciousness.

'The perfect man may stare at the blue heaven above, dive into the yellow springs below, ramble to the end of the eight directions, yet his spirit and *qi* (*shen qi* 神氣) undergo no change.'

Perfect beings are able to adapt to everything and remain unperturbed, they are not changed by external circumstances, not stirred by desires and so on. Here *shen qi* refers to all the *qi* that is activated within by the *shen*, and therefore all that one is and does. From the depths of the heart of wisdom, the spirits activate the *qi* and so the perfect being is wise in all things. This is because the spirits have embraced the way of heaven, the natural movement and evolution, and therefore the spirits of the perfect being are one with heaven. We find *shen qi* in the medical texts with almost the same meaning. In Suwen chapter 62, for example, excess and deficiency of spirits is seen as deficiency of the *qi* of the heart.

The inborn nature of a human being is to have the *shen* within. And to have the potential of making the *shen* bright or not, to enlighten them or not. *Ming* (明) is light, radiance, brightness, and is such an important concept to the Chinese. At the very beginning of the Great Learning is the idea of *ming ming de* (明 明 德) – to brighten radiant virtue. Virtue or vital powers (*de* 德) are part of our inborn nature, and also part of the integration with cosmic life. Within the human being, this is also related to a moral sensibility. These virtues are part of each human being, but it is up to us to make them bright. We must take care of them.

Question: Can you say something more about the ability to reach the spirits in treatment?

If we want to take care of the spirits, we cannot act as though we have no body. We are the body. But what is the 'I' that we are speaking of? This is discussed in some of the texts that we will look at later. I am what I am in my nature because of my body, the form given to me, and because of the spirits given to me. At the same time this conjunction of heaven and earth, essences and body, spirits and body, constitutes a human being with the specific qualities of being human, which are created by awareness. Through what is called heart/mind, which is my true self, I make what I receive bright or dull. And if I make it bright, I am bright. If I don't, I am dull. It is through the concentration of the *qi*, the way I regulate my life and calm the mind, that can I act in such a way that the spirits become efficacious. And this is also the means by which I can connect with others. That is the meaning of reaching the spirits.

We are able to reach the spirits with the needle, through the body. And also by looking into the eyes. This corresponds to the workings of heaven, and it is not something we can easily grasp or understand, but we all experience these things. It is not possible to probe or analyse this in the same way as we look at the complexion and take the pulses. The only way to be really healed is to change the way you act. The spirits will then activate the *qi* in a better, more harmonious way. If not, there may be a treatment, but it will not be a cure. Because unless the behaviour is changed, the problem will start again, in one way or another. It is not just a matter of burning incense and calling on the spirits of heaven to come into you! No! That is not to say that some rituals and prayers are not possible or even necessary. But it is the entire regulation of life that is important. And if I want to lead my life in calm quietness, perhaps that is what I need.

So what are the sages doing? Meditating. And what is meditation? It is not just sitting there, sleeping or dreaming. It is not something you learn in five minutes, by reading a do-it-yourself guide to meditation. It is difficult. It is a practice of many many years. And maybe gradually something begins to change. It is a way of life, to have rhythm and ritual within your life – in order to keep the body and mind clear and calm. They are able to get up at five o'clock in the morning – which is something that I have always admired immensely! Basically it is an extremely demanding practice. And it is not simply thinking about it, it is doing it.

JING 精 ESSENCES

Guanzi chapter 49: Neiye

'The vital essence in all beings is what makes them alive. Below, it produces the five grains. Above, it makes the stars and arranges them in order. Flowing (*liu* 流) into the space between heaven and earth, it is called *gui shen* (鬼 神, spirits of earth and heaven). Treasured (*cang* 藏) in the middle of the chest, we call it the sage (*sheng ren* 聖 人).'

This first sentence of chapter 49 is very important, because the Neiye is the most ancient text that we still have about the inner work (*nei ye* 內 業) of purifying oneself in order to refine essences and to be spirit-like. Having the best quality of essences and concentrating the *qi*, results in the presence of the spirits, and the presence of the spirits is nothing other than a kind of enlightenment.

This is the cosmic effect of the essences, the cosmic vitality which is the same everywhere – in heaven producing stars and on earth producing grains, and between heaven and earth, producing human beings. If essences are of the best quality, and this subtle vitality can be kept within the centre of the chest, or within the heart, then the spirits will be present. In other words, if life is guided by the great principles of the natural processes of life, enabling enlightened knowledge and a spiritual intelligence, this is called wisdom, or being a sage.

'…Aligned (*zheng* 正) and tranquil (*jing* 靜), there is stability (*ding* 定).'

This stability is not disturbed by anything, and does not undergo sudden change due to desires and passions which are not part of the natural evolution and transformation of life.

'If the heart/mind is stable within, the ears and eyes are sharp and clear (bright, *ming* 明) the four limbs are strong and firm, then there can be a dwelling place for the essences. The vital essence is the essences and *qi* (*jing qi* 精氣). When the *qi* is guided, there is renewal of life (*sheng* 生); with renewal of life there is thought (*si* 思), with thought there is knowledge (*zhi* 知), with knowledge there is a stop.'

If you have no way of stopping there will be excess. In Chinese to stop (*zhi* 止) is very close to *zheng* (正 correct, upright). With knowledge there is always a danger of going too far. We have to be able to stop, and not get caught up in knowledge, which is the same as being caught in desires.

We need to have essences, which constitute the very core of the vitality of a human being. This of course also implies sexual intercourse. The essences are the same thing in a man as sperm – the same character (*jing* 精) can be translated as sperm in certain contexts. For women it is the power of the essences in the blood within the uterus. We can see this in the second part of the Xici, chapter 2 line 5:

'Man and woman unite their essences (*jing* 精) and the ten thousand beings are produced through transformation (*hua sheng* 化生).'

This is the same process. When heaven and earth unite their essences, and when these essences, which contain the subtle pattern of life, are concentrated to make a form on earth, there is a being. When a man and woman unite their essences, there is the potential of a new being.

'It is ever so that in human life heaven produces vital essences (*jing* 精), earth produces form (*xing* 形). These combine to produce a human being. When they are in harmony there is life; without it, there is no life.'

This is the same for the spirits. If the spirits are present there is life, if they are not, there is death. Between spirit and harmony there is also an unavoidable link. The spirits prosper only through harmony and balance. So it is quite common in texts of this time to find the same kind of expression for both the spirits and the essences. We see at the end of Zhuangzi chapter 5:

'The way (*dao* 道) gave him (the sage) his external appearance, heaven gave him his bodily form (*xing* 形), he does not let likes or dislikes harm his being (*shen* 身). But you let the outside world dominate your spirit and toiling, wear out your vitality (*jing* 精). Leaning on a tree you mutter, propped up at your desk you doze. Heaven selected a body for you and you use it to babble on about the 'hard' and the 'white'.'

The hard and the white refers to all kinds of useless discussions and disputes about whether one thing is better than another. But it is not important to discuss these things because we just wear ourselves out. Burton Watson translates this beautifully as 'you treat your spirits as an outsider' not as something that you really incorporate into your own being, but treat as if it is some kind of tool. If you act in a certain way – you might think that you are brilliant, but it is in fact just pitiful. It is easy for us to get caught up in the brilliance of the mind – but what is the reality of that? Much of what is said here is relevant for our daily life and this Chinese way of thinking is important to awaken us to these things, and to place things in perspective. As for what is good for the spirits – it is always to keep quiet!

We see this again in Zhuangzi chapter 11:

'The essence (*jing* 精) of the perfect way is dark and obscure; the extremity of the perfect way is mysterious and hushed in silence. No seeing, no hearing; the spirit (*shen* 神) enfolded in quietude (*jing* 靜) – the body will align itself. Be still, be pure, do not labour your body (*xing* 形), do not churn up your essences (*jing* 精) and then there will be long life. When the eye does not see, the ear does not hear, and the mind (heart, *xin* 心) does not know, then your spirits (*shen* 神) will protect the body form (*xing* 形), and the body will enjoy long life.'

There is always the question, when translating a text, of using the singular or plural for spirit and essence. It is the same – but not the same – this essence which is found within the heavenly bodies, the five grains, or within us. The essence coming through us from food may be divided into the five tastes. It is the same thing – but it also different. It is the same for the spirits. If you take the spirits as all the influences from heaven that you may attract in your own body, how many are there? Are they one? Are they five, or one hundred? Are there eighteen thousand? Are there spirits of the spleen and the brain and the right eye, as we see in certain Daoist texts of later centuries? If we take spirit as one entity, we cannot speak of one spirit and one deity. There are thousands of spirits, but the myriad of spirits are also only one spirit, because all the spirits which activate life are also nothing other than the process of life itself, the processes of nature.

But there is also the identification of individual spirits – the spirit of the river, the spirit of the mountain and so on – and these spirits may even struggle between themselves. From a more philosophical perspective, all the spirits acting in the cosmos are in unity with the reality of life. And it is the same thing within each individual. So how many spirits do we have? Maybe myriads! But the spiritual illumination of my life is one. I do not have one spirit guiding my little finger and another in my left leg. It is not like that. So it is always possible to use the singular or plural. The important thing is to understand the meaning of the use of the singular and the meaning of the use of the plural. The singular is not to be taken as one spirit or deity, but as the unity, the oneness of all the activity of spirit.

Huainanzi chapter 7

> 'They share essences (*jing* 精) with the root of the great purity (*qing* 清), they roam about in the region of the indistinct. They have essences (*jing* 精) but do not use them up, they have spirits but do not overactivate them (*xing* 行). They have a pact with the primal simplicity of the great chaos and they stand in the centre of the perfect purity. Therefore, their sleep is without dreams, their wisdom does not burst forth; their *po* do not sink and their *hun* do not rise.'

We can see that unless we have the necessary quietness and calmness, the essences cannot remain clear and pure. There is a constant repetition of sound in these characters – *jing, qing, xing, ming* – which is very significant within the classical Chinese language.

Xunzi chapter 21

'The heart/mind (*xin* 心) is the ruler (*jun* 君) of the form (*xing* 形), and the master of spiritual illumination (*shen ming* 神 明). When the desires of ears and eyes assail it, they destroy thought. When the sound of mosquitoes or gnats is heard, it disturbs the essential spirits (*jing shen* 精 神).'

The heart is the ruler of the human body. The heart, the mind, is the self, the 'I'. But even the smallest thing can create disturbance; then the mind is no longer calm, and the essences are disturbed. Such a small thing is enough to disturb the essences, the vitality, the *qi*, and the vital spirits. The next day you cannot concentrate at work, because you did not sleep well, you are angry with your children, and at five o'clock the next day you do your practice – and after ten years maybe you will not be disturbed by mosquitoes! But we must not despair of human nature! This is the reality of the vital spirits. How can we be disturbed by so many things! To keep the spirits is to keep a real quietness; not one which is forced, but one which is deep.

Lüshi Chunqiu chapter 3 section II

This is a text from the middle of the 3rd century BCE:

'…For the essences and *qi* (*jing qi* 精 氣) to collect, there must be some place for them to enter. When essences collect in feathered birds, they can fly and swoop; when essences collect in animals with legs, they can support their weight and walk; when essences collect in pearls and jade, they are refined and clear; when they collect in trees and shrubs, they grow and are strong; when they collect in the sage, he is extremely brilliant (*ming* 明).'

The *qi* are undifferentiated, and in order to act specifically they must be within a form.

'When essences and *qi* (*jing qi* 精 氣) arrive: following what is light, they give flight; following what has legs, they give movement; following what has beauty, they make it fine; following what grows, they make it flourish; following what has consciousness, they make it brilliant (*ming* 明). The essences and *qi* rise and fall, turning and spreading out in a never-ending cycle.'

On a cosmic level, essences and *qi* are seen as all that is involved in making things as they are, each with its own characteristics and tendencies. They are specified by entering into a being or thing. The essences are the beginning of form, the *qi* is that which gives features to form. Within a human being, if one is has awareness, there will be illumination.

JING SHEN

Jing shen (精 神) can be seen as something external, which is also the case with *shen ming* (神 明) – as we have seen, *jing shen* are everywhere, in the tiniest autumn hair, or in the vast extent of the cosmos. And it is the same for us in fulfilment of our true human nature. Here, in Zhuangzi chapter 22, the *jing shen*, essences and spirits are born from the *dao*:

'The clear and bright is born from dark obscurity; order is born from the formless; essences and spirits (*jing shen* 精 神) are born from the way (*dao* 道); the original form is born from essences; and the ten thousand things produce one another.'

We will end with some quotes from chapter 7 of the Huainanzi, which is called Jing Shen.

'…The ten thousand beings then take form, coarse *qi* making insects, subtle *qi* (*jing qi* 精 氣) making humans. Therefore the vital spirits (*jing shen* 精 神) belong to heaven and the bony frame belongs to earth; the vital spirits re-enter the gate and the bony frame returns to its root. How can 'I' continue to exist?'

It is through the very features of the body that human beings are close to the image of the natural order and in harmony with heaven and earth. This is reflected in the way the body is formed, through gestation until at ten months it is born. Essences and *qi* make the human being in the likeness of the cosmic order, and it is not quite the same with other creatures. There is something within the body of a human being which suggests that its specific features reflect the order of heaven and earth. The human being is also able to govern; to rule with the mind. But the question is whether human beings are able to become spirit-like in their hearts, and not just indulge in mental power, which is an incomplete and distorted expression of the same potential of being spirit-like.

'…The *dao* of heaven and earth by its ultimate immensity is great, yet it moderates its display of light and cares for the radiance of the spirits (*shen ming* 神 明). How can the eyes and ears of man work long and hard without rest? How can the vital spirits (*jing shen* 精 神) race fast and furious without exhaustion?'

If the vital spirits do not simply follow the cosmic order, they will become exhausted.

'But when the vital spirits thrive and the *qi* are not scattered, then there is perfect order. Perfect order, then equilibrium; equilibrium, them free communication; free communication, then the spirits. With the spirits, in looking there is nothing that is not seen; in listening there is nothing that is not heard; in doing there is nothing that is not accomplished. Thus worries and concerns cannot enter, and perverse *qi* cannot strike.'

According to our behaviour, we enhance or damage the vital spirits. And of course they can never be separated from the body.

'They are present as if vanished and live as if dead; they enter and leave where there is no opening, use ghosts and spirits as servants; they are engulfed by the unfathomable and enter into what has no opening, in order to be moulded into different forms. Endings and beginnings are like a circle, no-one can grasp their succession. This is how the vital spirits are able to merge with the *dao*.'

SHEN AND JING SHEN IN MEDICAL TEXTS

Suwen chapter 5

'The Yellow Emperor said: *Yin yang* is the way of heaven and earth, the laws and principles of the ten thousand beings, father and mother of change and transformation, root and beginning of life and death, dwelling place of the radiant spirits (*shen ming* 神明).'

Here *shen ming* (神明) is the harmony of all transformations, all beginnings and endings and all that presides over them. It is also that which is in the sanctuary in the centre of the chest – the heart/mind.

At the beginning of the central part of Suwen chapter 5, where there is a presentation on each of the five elements, in the section on the eastern quarter and the wood we see:

'In heaven it is the dark mystery (*xuan* 玄), in human beings it is the way (*dao* 道); on earth it is transformation (*hua* 化). Transformation produces the five tastes, the way produces wisdom, and the dark mystery produces the spirits (*shen* 神). The spirits, in heaven are the wind, on earth wood…'

Everything is the spirits, but here we see their manifestation in heaven and on earth. Also, later in the same chapter:

'Thus, heaven through its essences (*jing* 精) and earth through its forms (*xing* 形), heaven through the eight regulators of time and earth through the five organizers (five elements, phases, *wu xing* 五行) can act as father and mother of the ten thousand beings.'

It is through the meeting of heaven and earth that everything is made, and here, essences from heaven are the vitality of life within any form; earth gives the form. Essences and spirits are the cosmic aspect of life and are linked with heaven, the specific form with its distinct attributes is related to earth.

'Since clear *yang* rises to heaven and turbid *yin* returns to earth, heaven and earth move and are still, the radiant spirits (*shen ming* 神 明) form the net of laws and principles. Thus through a process of generating, growing, gathering and burying, everything reaches its term and starts again.'

Here is the complete vision of the radiant spirits, or spiritual illumination – as all the various kinds of transformation which produce life between heaven and earth, with the laws and principles, the order which is always present. Generating, growing, gathering and burying are the laws and cycles of nature as seen in the four seasons.

Suwen chapter 1

In the medical texts, the vital spirits are mainly referred to by their presence within the individual, where they are necessary for a complete human life. At the end of Suwen chapter 1 there is a description of the authentic human being (*zhen ren* 真 人), the perfect human being (*zhi ren* 至 人) and the sage (*sheng ren* 聖 人), and in each case their authenticity is linked to the vital spirits (*jing shen* 精 神), or the essences and *qi* (*jing qi* 精 氣).

> 'At the time of high antiquity, there were authentic human beings (*zhen ren* 真 人) who grasped heaven and earth, held *yin* and *yang* in their hands, and breathed with the essences and *qi* (*jing qi* 精 氣). They established this within themselves by keeping the spirits (*shen* 神).'

> 'In the time of middle antiquity there were perfect human beings (*zhi ren* 至 人); candid in their virtue, perfect in the way, animated by *yin yang*, balanced by the four seasons. Having left the ordinary world, they gathered essences (*jing* 精) and looked after the integrity of the spirits (*shen* 神). They wandered freely in the space between heaven and earth.'

> 'Next there were the sages, (*sheng ren* 聖 人); they adopted the harmonized *qi* of heaven and earth, and adapted themselves to the regular course of the eight winds; exposed to the desires and passions of the world, they did not feel irritation or anger. …Their body in perfect condition, they retained their vital spirits (*jing shen* 精 神). Thus it was possible for them to reach one hundred years of age.'

Lingshu chapter 71

> 'The heart is the great master of the five *zang* and the six *fu*. It is the dwelling place of the vital spirits (*jing shen* 精 神). When this is solid and firm, the perverse influences cannot penetrate. If they penetrate then the heart is affected. If the heart is affected the spirits leave. If the spirits leave it is death.'

Here the spirits are the vitality. If the vitality is not there, there is no life. But there can be another understanding of the spirits, even in the medical texts, where there is an expression of the spirits, but they are dull. Life continues, even if the light of the spirits is not present, but the vitality will be damaged day after day, and will become more and more sensitive to perverse influences. Similarly in Suwen chapter 13:

> 'To possess the spirits (*de shen* 得 神) is the splendour (*chang* 昌) of life, loss of the spirits (*shi shen* 失 神) is ruin (*wang* 亡).'

And in Lingshu chapter 54:

> 'At one hundred years the five *zang* are all empty and the *shen qi* (神 氣) are gone. Only the body frame remains.'

The spirits also represent the functioning of the mind and the intellect, through their relationship with the heart/mind (*xin* 心). The *qi* is activated by the spirits, which will no longer be present when the five *zang* are exhausted. At one hundred years, what was given at the beginning of life is exhausted and by taking care of the essences, one fulfils one's allotted years.

THE SPIRITS AND THE HEART

In the medical texts the spirits are linked to the heart. We see this in Suwen chapter 8, where the heart is presented as the lord and master, and the light of the spirits radiates from the heart:

'The heart holds the office of sovereign and master and the radiance of the spirits (*shen ming* 神 明) stems from it.'

And in Lingshu chapter 8:

'The heart stores the vital circulation (*mai* 脈) and the *mai* are the dwelling place of the spirits.'

This is the double aspect of the heart – functioning both through the mind and consciousness and in the circulation of the blood – which is also a dwelling place for the spirits. The presence of the spirits in the heart is the core of who I am. So even in this context they are essentially linked with all evolution, change and transformation. We saw the same thing with the *shen ming* in relation to the cosmos, where they were linked with the cyclical movement of life throughout the four seasons, the metamorphoses and transformation of the *yin yang*. That can also be seen in Suwen chapter 9:

'The heart is the root of life, (*sheng zhi ben* 生 之 本) transformation is operated by the spirits.'

Similarly in Lingshu chapter 69:

'When one speaks of transformation (*hua* 化), it is nothing other than communing with the natural order, with the principles of life (*li* 理) through communication with the light of the spirits (*shen ming* 神 明).'

Change and transformation come about through the communication with the *shen ming*, the light of the spirits. And it is through the *shen ming* that we are able to change and transform according to the appropriate time and the right circumstances – which is, of course, all part of good health. The title of Suwen chapter 2 is the 'Great Treatise on How the Four Qi Harmonize and Regulate the Spirits' (*si qi tiao shen da lun* 四氣調神大論). The four *qi* (*si qi* 四氣) are the *qi* of the four seasons. Do they regulate the spirits, or do the spirits regulate them? At a subtle level, the spirits manifest themselves in the *shen ming*, the splendour, the beauty of the universe. And the best example of this, which is always referred to, is the succession and unfolding of the four seasons. In the cosmos, what we may call spirit manifests itself through the natural order.

As a human being, I take this as an example, and by observing the four seasons I am able to understand more about the natural order. In following the natural order, I use the power of my own awareness, in order to follow and adapt myself – my body, my thoughts and my behaviour – to the changes of the seasons. I am therefore able to regulate the expression of the spirits within me by following this change in the natural order.

We adapt ourselves and our behaviour by following the natural order, and in so doing, we are able to become more and more spirit-like. It is simply a way of following the *qi* of each season and of nourishing life, which is to be the companion of the natural order. That is also the way to achieve what we call the correct or upright *qi* (*zheng qi* 正氣). If I adjust my behaviour according to the *qi* of each season, I nourish the spirits, but I also nourish the correct *qi* – which includes the correct defence (*wei* 微). I do not allow thoughts and feelings inappropriate to the season to arise, and do not to allow perverse *qi* to enter. As we see in Suwen chapter 1:

'The sages of antiquity educated their subjects, speaking to them in this way: Emptiness, perverse influences (*xie qi* 邪氣) and robber winds are avoided by taking account of the season. In peaceful calm, void and emptiness, the authentic *qi* (*zhen qi* 真氣) flow easily, essences and spirits (*jing shen* 精神) are kept within. How could illness arise?'

To model oneself on the spirits from heaven allows the highest possible functioning of life at all levels – mental, emotional, physical – and is consequently the best prevention of disease and the best way to build immunity. This is the reason why the quality of the spirits of the heart is linked with the quality and strength of the correct *qi* (*zheng qi* 正氣). In Lingshu chapter 3 we see that the great acupuncturist is concerned with the spirits:

'The main things concerning the practice with fine needles are not difficult to explain; what is difficult is a deep understanding. The good practitioner guards the body, the great acupuncturist guards the spirits. But if we are unable to examine and know all the aspects of the disease, how can we understand and know the origin of the disease.'

There follows an explanation of making a diagnosis and also the way to insert the needle into 'emptiness', into the void, in order to obtain a result. Lingshu chapter 3 says that the crude practitioner guards the body, which means the techniques of needling. This is quite something, but not enough. To guard the spirits means to guard the blood and *qi*. We must not forget that blood and *qi* are always related to the spirits, as we see in Lingshu chapter 18:

'Nutrition and defence, *ying wei* (營衛) are essences and *qi* (*jing qi*

精氣). As for the blood, it is spirit *qi* (*shen qi* 神氣).'

And Suwen chapter 26:

'Blood and *qi* are the spirits of man.'

That the superior physician guards the spirits, means that he guards the blood and *qi* – which are nothing other than the expression of the spirits. We cannot see the spirits, but by perceiving the balance and the harmony of blood and *qi* we know the spirits, tonifying or dispersing according to excess or deficiency. This is what we saw in the Xici; by observing transformation within the universe we also are able to know the spirits.

When speaking of 'the spirit and the guest', as in Lingshu chapter 3, the texts are referring to the perverse *qi* and the correct *qi*. The spirits are the correct *qi*, the guests at the door are the perverse, looking for a way to enter. The spirits are the best expression of life, but also the guardian of life and death. This also implies the quality of everything that makes up nutrition and defence, so when the spirits are present, and when I recognize that I am more and more spirit-like, everything functions well because the *qi* are activated and guided by an undisturbed mind.

If you guard the spirits, the spirits will guard and protect you – by guarding all the doors where unwelcome guests might try to enter. The spirits protect through the blood and *qi*, and through all that is maintained by the five *zang*, etc. The ability of the spirits to protect is maintained through the quiet stillness of the mind. This enables the efficiency of the vital spirits. The door are the pores, the orifices, and maybe even the acupuncture points.

This is something that we can find expressed more completely in

Nanjing Difficulty 8:

'The twelve meridians (*jing mai* 經脈) are connected to the source (*yuan* 原) of the vital *qi* (*sheng qi* 生氣). The source of the vital *qi* is the root and foundation (*gen ben* 根本) of the twelve meridians, that is the *qi* moving between the kidneys (*shen jian dong qi* 腎間動氣). This *qi* is the foundation of the five *zang* and the six *fu*, the root of the twelve meridians, the gate of exhalation and inhalation, the source (*yuan* 原) of the triple heater. They are also called the guardian of the spirits against perverse influences (*shou xie zhi shen* 守邪之神).'

The maintenance of the natural functioning, the heavenly work in all the five *zang*, six *fu*, twelve meridians, the breath and so on, is the natural order within me, and this is nothing other than the presence of the spirits. It is also the way to refuse entry to the unwanted guests at the doors. Hence the *qi* constitutes a person's root and foundation. The correct *qi* is not really different from what we call the spirits – as an effect and also as a cause. The spirits are nothing other than what I am.

This is also seen in an interesting quotation from Lingshu chapter 32:

'For an ordinary man, when the stomach is filled (*man* 滿) the intestine is empty (*xu* 虛), and when the intestine is filled, the stomach is empty. Because they are empty and full alternately, the *qi* ascend and descend, the five *zang* are peaceful and stable, the blood circulates with harmony and ease; hence the vital spirits (*jing shen* 精神) dwell in their residence. Therefore the spirits are the essences and *qi* (*jing qi* 精氣) coming from water and grains.'

Without the support of the physical forces, there is no *qi* and therefore no vitality (or essences) for the spirits. The strength of the mind is lacking – there is no power in thought and decision making. This is a good example of the complete interaction and intermingling of body and spirits in our day to day lives. But it does not imply that the one who has built a true spiritual inner life will lose that if there is not enough food to eat. This kind of spirituality is at a different level to the mental capacity referred to here.

There are several explanations of techniques of needling, for example in Suwen chapter 27, where there are techniques to tonify, by palpation, massage and so on – we try to close the doors, in order to keep the spirits within. We close the doors because through these doors there may be a kind of scattering and dispersal of *qi*, which is the same thing as the lack of spirits. And, as we have seen, blood and *qi* are also awareness, consciousness and perception – the way that I react. If my blood and *qi* are not full of the consciousness of the spirits, I am unable to distinguish hot and cold, pain and pleasure, and I can be startled with fright by anything that is unexpected. Just because something is unexpected, it is not a reason to be disturbed. Sometimes we can be disturbed by the expected – but if the blood and *qi* which comes from the vital spirits in the heart, are settled, then I am not disturbed. There may be a mosquito, or a sudden noise, but I do not move. But if I move suddenly, there is a scattering of *qi*, which is also a sign of a scattering of spirits. Here we are talking about the spirits not as the spirits of heaven, but as my own awareness – my ability to concentrate the mind which is no longer stable. As we saw in the Neiye – the spirits are disturbed and the heart is no longer stable.

The manipulation indicated for the needle allows the *qi* to arrive; to keep it, we close the doors so that the spirits and *qi* remain and act within, as they must. So the needling technique will be dependent on what is required. If we calm the mind, concentrate the *qi*, the spirits are more real. They guide the *qi* according to the movement and circulation proper to each individual life. That is what we do with patients, and also with our friends. We help them to calm down and concentrate, which enables them to be more themselves.

In Suwen chapter 62 and Suwen chapter 27 there is a discussion on the way to needle in a case of excess or insufficiency of the spirits. The text says that we must take care of the circulation and the blood and *qi* of the heart, the correct *qi* of the heart. Are they weak or are they racing wildly, as we saw in the Huainanzi – 'when the vital spirits race fast and furious out of bounds'. Are the *qi* of the heart racing fast and furious? Or are they weak and insufficient? We must work on what we find within the blood and *qi* and in this context this is called an excess or insufficiency of the spirits. This must be seen within the specific context of this chapter, where for each of the five *zang*, there is one representative, for example an excess or insufficiency of will for the kidneys. It is always the context which gives the level of understanding. In Suwen chapter 62 we cannot take the insufficiency of the *shen* as if it were the cosmic *shen* or the potentiality of each human being to become like the cosmic *shen* and to build the vital spirits in the likeness of heaven. This is not the same level of interpretation. Here the *shen* represent the functioning of the heart, and the way in which the heart/mind is able to assure the correct functioning of the circulation of blood.

Quite often in the medical texts the *jing shen* (精 神), the *shen* (神) or the *shen ming* (神 明) are linked with the intelligence which enables us to make the correct diagnosis. Suwen chapters 13 and 17 present a similar idea. The intelligence within me is the same as the spiritual brightness, which is the natural order of life. And being a part of that, my eyes are able to see and there is nothing which is not seen. I can perceive all the signs shown by the patient, classify them, and also know the correct treatment.

In Suwen chapter 17, there is the question not only of the *shen ming* (神明) but also *jing ming* (精明), the brightness of the essences – or the light which comes from the purity and clarity of the essences. If my essences are pure and clear, it is because of my behaviour – I nourish my heart and my self with what is required for them to thrive, with harmony and whatever is congenial to my life. In this case it is the presence of the spirits, which is also the perfect functioning of the five *zang*, which offer essences to the heart, make up the perfect quality of the blood and the perfect harmony between blood and *qi*. It is all the same thing.

At the end of Suwen chapter 26 we can see the same thing. *Shen ming* (神明) is in the title of the chapter:

> 'This is why to maintain (to nourish) the life of the spirits it is necessary to know the state of repletion or emaciation of the body; the rising of power or the decline of blood and *qi*. The blood and *qi* are the spirits of a human being. One cannot but pay attention to their maintenance.'

To know the state of the spirits, it is necessary to look at the body, to look at the blood and *qi*, nutrition and defence; all the *yin yang* expression of life. After this section, we are told how to proceed according to the repletion or emaciation, fullness and emptiness, through the quality of the spirits. The spirits are what allows the eyes to see clearly, the heart to be open and the will to be full of wisdom, and therefore to be able to understand the reality of things. It is to go from the signs to the cause, through all the various effects in the body. By looking at the exterior signs we know what is happening to the blood and *qi*, nutrition and defence; we also know that this comes from the vital spirits of the individual, and is dependent on whether they are able to build their vitality in the right way.

Suwen chapter 80 refers to the behaviour of the practitioner:

'The great principle of diagnosis is that the practitioner must be able to rule their own behaviour, and understand all the manipulations of the needle (to enter and come out) and master all these movements in order to make the *shen ming* (神 明 spiritual brightness) function correctly. It is necessary to purify oneself, to clarify oneself, in order to observe what is above and what is below.'

To understand diagnosis, it is necessary for the practitioner to have the vital spirits (*jing shen* 精 神) or radiance of the spirits (*shen ming* 神 明) functioning fully and well – this will open the eyes, give sensitivity to the fingers (in palpation and specifically feeling the pulse where the practitioner feels the blood and *qi* of the patient and therefore the spirits), give accuracy to the hearing, and so on.

'The eyes are where the heart and the spirits are present… the ears are where the essences of the kidneys are enlightened by the spirits.'
(Lingshu chapter 80)

The treatment must reach the spirits; not to go directly, but through the blood and *qi*, through nutrition and defence, through the twelve meridians and the five *zang*, in order to reorganize the *qi* and to help the concentration in such a way that the patient is able to come back to him or herself. Then the functioning of the *qi*, the quality of the heart/mind and the vital spirits will manifest the true brightness of the vision of reality and a better integration of one's life and the natural order. That is a real treatment, and it is accomplished by the patient – though they may not be aware of that. The level of consciousness is not necessarily important here, it depends on the circumstances. If the treatment is effective, it is done by the patient, even if they are not aware of it. Inner transformation is achieved by the spirits – the spirits allow the implementation of healing.

Jing shen is of course related to the heart, but also to all the five *zang*, because the five *zang* are the perfect functioning of the heart, and the quality of the blood and *qi* depends on the function of all the organs. Certainly all the five *zang* with their individual expression of the spirits play a role in the harmony and consistency of what we call our vital spirits. The most important thing is always harmony. We see this in Lingshu chapter 54:

'Huangdi asked, What makes the spirits?

'Qi Bo replied: When blood and *qi* are in harmony, when nutrition and defence (*ying wei* 營 衛) commune and circulate freely, when the five *zang* are perfectly achieved, then the *shen qi* (神 氣) dwells in the heart. *Hun* and *po* are complete with all their capacities, and this perfect achievement is a human being.'

The text always comes back to blood and *qi*, nutrition and defence and their perfect harmony; the *qi*, acting through the impulse of the spirits, are in the heart. Suwen chapter 14 presents the same idea; this is a situation in which a patient is weak and the blood is exhausted, and the treatment gives no result. The Emperor asks why that is the case. Qi Bo answers that the spirits are no longer acting, sending messages or giving orders.

'The Emperor asks: What does it mean that the spirits are no longer acting (*shi* 使)?

Qi Bo replies: When you practise the way of the needles, if the vital spirits (*jing shen* 精 神) cannot move forward, if the will and intent (*zhi yi* 志 意) do not rule, then the illness cannot be cured.'

There must be a change within the inner disposition (*zhi yi* 志 意) for an illness to be cured. The will and intent are an expression of the heart; they rule the inner life, and so designate the vital spirits. If the vital spirits (*jing shen* 精 神) do not move forward, it means that they do not activate the cure.

'When the essences (*jing* 精) are damaged and the spirits (*shen* 神) are gone, nutrition and defence (*ying wei* 營 衛) cannot recover their place. Desire and covetousness know no limits; worries and concerns are endless. Essences and *qi* (*jing qi* 精 氣) are loose and damaged. Nutrition is stagnant, defence is absent, so the spirits being gone, the illness cannot be cured.'

Here the spirits are absent but the patient is still living; it is the 'spirit-likeness' that is gone. The reality of the vital spirits always comes back to what I do with my will and intent (*zhi yi* 志 意); what I allow to inhabit my heart. In Suwen chapter 3 we see the same thing, that it is the harmonious regulation according to time and season, which allows perverse influences to be avoided.

'What is essential for *yin yang* comes down to this: solidity (*gu* 固) depends on whether the *yang* are well-sealed (*mi* 密). A lack of harmonious composition between the two will be like spring without autumn, winter without summer. Such is the rule of the sages. But if the *yang* are too powerful, and cannot be kept tightened, the *yin qi* are interrupted. If the *yin* are steady and the *yang* well-sealed, the vital spirits (*jing shen* 精 神) are as controlled as they can be; but if there is separation and rupture, disharmony between *yin* and *yang* occurs, essences and *qi* (*jing qi* 精 氣) are interrupted.'

The link with the body is of course very important. It is always through the body that we see the effect of the spirits. There may also be a specific effect on the spirits of the patient, but this comes from the patient. We see in Lingshu chapter 30:

'When two spirits (*shen* 神) embrace, their union gives form to a body. What comes first is called essences (*jing* 精).'

The essences are always the beginning of form. But in this text, the *shen* presides over the concentration and union of essences at the beginning of the formation of the body. Once there is the beginning of a body-form, this form is able to welcome the *qi* and welcome the spirits. But the spirits also give the awareness that enables a human being to manage and govern individual life. Heaven bestows the natural order and the rhythm of the four seasons; earth the richness and the ability to grow. Within the human being there is the potential to rule through the heart, or through the will and intent (*zhi yi* 志 意), which are the inner disposition of the heart, and two of the *wu shen* (五 神) or five aspects of spirit. Because of this potential, it is possible for human beings to build the vital spirits within themselves. And this building of the vital spirits and the ability to govern (*zhi* 治) determines what we are, the way we think, the way we perceive, the way we act, and gives us the ability to make a diagnosis and to treat accordingly.

Of course, essences and spirits within medicine are also the kidneys and the heart – the link between the origin and the manifestation, the governing of life, which must proceed according to the inborn nature. This is necessary if we want to become spirit-like, through the constant rebuilding of the vital spirits. The meaning of *yuan shen* (元 神), which is also found in daoist texts, is that the spirits maintain the relationship with the origin. Depending on the context, this can be seen at different levels. The first is to understand the spirits as the root of the manifestation of destiny (*ming* 命), and to adhere to the inborn nature (*xing* 性), which is the principle of each individual body and life, and also the way to participate with the spirits and essences of the cosmos. But it is also the mental calm and stability of the mind which allows the fulfilment of destiny. This is linked to the heart. It is the vital spirits as the total activity of the heart/mind – the spiritual life, the foundation of thought, consciousness and awareness, and the conduct which comes from that, and which leads to the diminution of desire and passion.

Another very specific meaning of *yuan shen* is in relationship to the brain, which is called *yuan shen zhi fu* (元 神 之 府), the dwelling place of the original spirit. Here it facilitates the good functioning of the brain. Through the sense organs and the communication with the heart, *yuan shen* (元 神) is the way of manifesting a connection with the reality of the cosmic spirits.

ASPECTS OF SPIRIT

yi zhi

YI ZHI 意 志

Intent (*yi* 意) and will (*zhi* 志) are two of the five aspects of spirit (*wu shen* 五神) in Chinese medicine, but it is not easy to understand why they are called 'spirits'. And why are the terms *zhi* and *yi* so important when attempting to understand the functioning of the mind, sometimes even representing the whole function of the heart/mind (*xin* 心)? By looking at the use of these characters in the classical texts both around and before the time of the elaboration of the theory of medicine, we can begin to formulate an understanding of these terms and see how they have been used at different times and in different contexts. In medicine, the five spirits are linked to the five *zang*, in an application of the theory of the five elements, but we will see that *yi* and *zhi* are very important concepts in the classical texts, and their meaning is often more than will and intent.

The character yi

The character for *yi* (意), is made with the heart (心) and above that a mouth, with something issuing from it, which is a sound, but a sound which is modulated. This character (*yin* 音) is also used for the five musical notes, and it represents a variation of sound, like the voice, which changes according to circumstances, but also according to what is in the heart. It is an expression of what is in the heart, which changes and is modified by the heart and the mind. If I am happy, I will sing and make joyful music; if I am sad I will sing a sad song. And if I have a kind of military temperament, I may sing a military march. So the character suggests a sound, but a sound modulated by the temperament, a sound which reflects the condition of the heart.

Yi (意) is an intent, an idea, a feeling that the person emitting the sound holds within them, and the character is used widely in Chinese to express the individual temperament; it is a way of thinking – but not the same kind of thought processes that are linked with the spleen in the medical texts. *Yi* refers to ideas that are in the heart and mind, that which gives me the impetus to speak as I speak. It is the meaning that I give to things, and the way I understand things and react to them. I react to things, and to people, according to my understanding of them, and the constructions within my heart/mind.

In Chinese, *yi* (意) expresses the fundamental attribute of awareness, it is the way in which I am aware and understand – the way I deduce the meaning of something. I have a feeling, an idea and an opinion, but there is also something which exists before the elaboration of thinking. For example, when someone is discussing, arguing and defending their ideas, they have already built some kind of understanding and preconceptions in their heart. And that is developed through education, life experience, etc. Both what I think and what I say do not come from 'nowhere'. There is always something within the depths of my being which creates the texture of my mind.

The *yi* (意) is the first stage of this reaction within the heart – the mental disposition and ability – because it is not possible to have a thought unless there is something upon which to build that thought. I can only elaborate thinking if I have some kind of perception, and can develop that perception, and give that perception some kind of orientation. I may be irritated by the situation, and that irritation will influence all my thoughts and reactions, and all the decisions that I make.

So *yi* is the beginning of what we may call intention, and also the beginning of will, *zhi* (志), as we see in Lingshu chapter 8, (cf: The Heart in Lingshu chapter 8). In certain contexts we find that *yi* and *zhi* are almost interchangeable. What is present in my mind is already a kind of determination.

If, for example, I am irritable, I expect something to nourish my irritation. So in this case the *yi* is seen as a kind of preconception. Before I am able to conceive of something in my mind, there is something less formed that the heart can work on and work with – and this is the *yi*. The mind is a working process, but it has to work on something. The *yi* allows this activity of the mind to begin. It is the first movement of the mind when the awareness is called towards something.

For example, if I am walking down the street and I pass a shop which sells chocolate cake – my reaction is an action of *yi* – an interest is awakened, and it attracts the attention of my heart/mind, and I begin to formulate something, because now I have the chocolate cake in my mind. Here the *yi* is a kind of sketch, a first outline of what will later become the more elaborate functioning of the mind, mixing information and desire. Desire becomes will – and when I see the chocolate cake I receive the information that here is a big delicious chocolate cake, but it cannot be separated from my reaction. The heart/mind mixes together the mental ability of human thought with decision making and planning, desire, passion and emotion – and all that is mixed with perception and information. These are the cognitive and volitive facets of the heart or of the *yi*.

Yi suggests that there is a predisposition, because if I have something in my mind it creates a predisposition towards something. If I continue to think about the chocolate cake, I will have a predisposition to look for chocolate cake everywhere, it becomes part of the process of my mind. The *yi* is at the very basis of the functioning of the heart/mind.

The most important point here is that we must be aware of what we allow into the heart/mind. The chocolate cake is already in my mind, but I can try to get rid of this image by trying not to think about it, or taking a different route to work. Or I can continue to see it every morning, and it will occupy more and more of my thoughts. But I am responsible for what I allow into my mind – just as every evening I am responsible for turning off the TV if I am watching a stupid film! We may tell ourselves that it is of no importance, but it is nourishing our mind, in one way or another. As Mencius said, if everyday you go to the area of the dyers, where there is a very strong smell of dye, don't be surprised if after a few weeks you smell of dye yourself! We expose ourselves to these things, whether it is the thought of chocolate cake, or watching rubbish on television, and it all contributes to the building of our inner disposition. It nourishes the heart, and therefore influences the forms that are taken by the mind. Its influence pervades all my actions, thoughts, temperament and desires. And of course, advertising plays on all of that.

So we must be careful of what we allow into our minds. We must be aware of what we see and what we hear, because it enters into our being. The heart/mind receives all the information from the sense organs – so it is not simply that the function of the heart/mind depends on what I see and hear, but more on what I allow my ears and eyes to receive.

YI IN CLASSICAL TEXTS

In the Chunqiu Zuozhuan, a prince had three officials to take care of what entered his senses. The first provided good balanced food, because the tastes are responsible for the renewal of *qi*. Another official was responsible for what the prince would see, and another for what he would hear. And in the 3rd century BCE there is a text which claims that music can lead to debauchery. What enters through the ear affects the mind, leading to desires of this or that. So we are responsible for what we think and we need to pay attention to what is at the root of our thinking. The only way to avoid bad thinking is to go to its root. And the root of thinking is the *yi*.

In order to recognize the root of bad thinking or an inappropriate desire, it is necessary to recognize what kind of situation, place, relationship, has contaminated you, and made you think in that way. The only way to do that is to cultivate yourself, by choosing things which are beneficial: nourishing yourself with good reading, looking at what allows the mind to see the natural order of things, meditating on the meaning of the regular succession of the four seasons, and on natural phenomena, and the order in which they arise, and so on. This is the correct nourishment of the mind which, little by little, allows you to see things correctly, and according to the natural order of life. The heart will then function in the same way as the movement of life – which is to be like Confucius at the age of 70, when he was able to follow the desire of his heart without transgressing any natural laws.

A good Confucian, cultivates himself, and is careful to nourish his mind with the right things. Not to know too much – because knowledge for the sake of knowledge was not even valued by Confucius! He said that even if a man knows the Book of Odes by heart, it is not a reason for me to admire him! So it is more the idea of behaving harmoniously, in a way which is consistent with the development of life in the universe.

Daxue, The Great Learning

The Daxue is a text which was studied in order to gain entry into the Great School. It is a very short text, but it was chosen in the Song dynasty as one of the four texts which form the Confucian Canon. Generation after generation of scholars learnt it by heart.

> 'The way of great learning teaches the illumination of brilliant virtue (*ming ming de* 明明德) to renew the people and to rest in the highest excellence.'

De (德) is virtue or vital power; it is not to be virtuous in a moral sense, but to follow the natural pattern of life, to have an awareness of the order of life and to behave accordingly. In this case it is to be perfect and to be highly efficient, because it is to work with the nature of things and not against them. This is the same as developing one's own vital power. Ming (明) is brightness, intelligence, cleverness, etc. So here, *ming ming de* is to illuminate (*ming* 明) brilliant virtue (*ming de* 明德). This means that within each human being there is an ability to build awareness. Each person has, through their own nature, a kind of vital power, the possibility to become aware of this power, and an understanding of the way to follow it. Each human being has a heart/mind which is intelligent and bright enough to see the natural order of life and the organization which is within each being and each phenomenon. Being aware of that, it is possible to mould the heart and behaviour, and become more and more virtuous, more and more sage-like, more and more spiritual. This is *shen ming* (神明) – spiritual awareness, or spiritual illumination. This is not only the ability to understand, which is the function of the heart/mind, but also to be aware of the reality of life, and at the same time to have the desire to be at one with this reality of life. The spirits of heaven are a kind of model, and as the functioning of the heart/mind, the spirits within the individual heart will become the same as the spirits of heaven. That is the accomplishment of human destiny.

This is important for the understanding of *yi* and *zhi* because it is the function of the heart. *Yi* and *zhi* are the very basis of the function of the heart/mind, and it is through the function of the heart that I am able to come back to my true nature or to return to a behaviour which is increasingly real. This is stated at the very beginning of the text. The great learning shows the way to promote illustrious virtue (*ming ming de* 明明德), to renew oneself every day, which is something that we find in many Confucian texts. If you are a good Confucian, you examine yourself every day, to see what is wrong within your thinking and desires – and then try to eradicate that, as you would remove weeds from a garden. But of course, if you do not get rid of the root, tomorrow it will just come back again. It is an endless process which never stops.

> 'The ancients, who wished to illuminate brilliant virtue throughout the world, first ordered (*zhi* 治) their own states. Wishing to order their own states, they first regulated their families... Wishing to cultivate themselves, they first rectified their hearts; wishing to rectify their hearts, they first sought to be sincere in their thoughts (*yi* 意). Wishing to be sincere in their thoughts (*yi* 意) they first extended their knowledge to the utmost... Their knowledge being complete, their thoughts (*yi* 意) were sincere. Their thoughts being sincere, their hearts were rectified...'

This is a very important text, which is pure Confucianism, and one of the basic texts of Confucian teaching. Governing well (*zhi* 治) is to govern by putting things back into their natural order, and it is the same character that is used with the meaning of treating or curing in medicine. It is also widely used in the context of governing *zhi* (志) and *yi* (意), as it is through the *zhi* and the *yi* that it is possible to put the mind in order.

If you want to bring order to the world, you must first know how to govern your kingdom. In order to do that, you have to show that you understand the way things work – in the way that Yu the Great was able to control the flood water and then govern the empire by showing that he understood the nature of things. He did not force the water to be raised up by building levees and dykes. Instead he helped the water to follow its own nature by digging canals and ditches for it to descend to the sea, because the nature of water is to descend. Having shown that he was able to understand the nature of things, and act in such a way that allowed things to proceed according to their own nature, Yu was entrusted with the government of the world, and he became emperor. Here the character *zhi* (治) is used for 'to govern', but is also used for the regulation of water by Yu the Great. If you want to rule, you have to show that you understand the basic principles of rulership, which is to know the nature of things. Yu the Great literally controlled the waters by putting an end to their destructive disorder and reinstating their life-giving and life maintaining flow.

In this text ordering the state is compared to putting your family in order, which is never easy. The Emperor Shun had a completely dysfunctional family! – a crazy brother, a useless father and a mother who was said to be a witch. Emperor Yao considered Shun to be exceptional because he had managed to create some kind of order in this very dysfunctional family. To ensure that he would be a good governor, he sent him his two daughters as wives – and Shun became the Emperor. Anyone reading these texts in China would know the stories of Yao and

Shun by heart, and therefore their implications.

If you are capable of putting your family in order, it is a sign that you know how to rule. But in order to put your family in order, you must work on yourself first. This is exactly what we see nowadays in psychoanalysis – if one has a dysfunctional family, one has to work on oneself. It is not by working from the outside, but by working on oneself – by cultivating oneself – that change can be effected. If you are in a better state, you not only know how to organize things around you, but that which emanates from you helps to create order. It is the same thing in treatment.

In order to cultivate oneself, the first thing is to cultivate the heart – to rectify the heart/mind, to guide it in the right direction. The heart can be rectified by working on the *yi*, and by making the *yi* sincere (*cheng* 誠) and perfectly accomplished (*cheng* 成). Here the *yi* becomes accomplished through the thorough investigation of things and beings. This of course is very Confucian too. It is in the study of good books (those of the sage) and of nature. This is the way to nourish oneself day after day. Gradually the *yi* becomes more real, closer to the reality of life. Your understanding is better, not because you are more clever or intelligent, or have an accumulation of knowledge, but because you have more of an understanding of the reality of things. The functioning of the heart/mind will be rectified. You will be upright. And of course, this is an endless process. If you cultivate yourself, then the family is in better order and the kingdom is well regulated and everyone in the world will be happy to be governed by you.

This text shows the importance and meaning of *yi* (意), and how it is at the root of the functioning of the heart/mind.

Guanzi Neiye

The Neiye is chapter 49 of the Guanzi, and is very different from the rest of the work. It is part of the four chapters on inner life, the cultivation of the mind and the art of the heart. In this chapter, which is called inner workings, the *yi* appears several times. I like Rickett's translation of *yi* (意) as the power of awareness, which is certainly one aspect of *yi*. It may be translated as intent, intention, thought, ideas, and all may be correct, depending on the context.

'Thus, the *qi* can not be restrained by physical strength, but may be calmed by the vital power (*de* 德). It will never come to one's call, but may be welcomed by one's power of awareness (*yi* 意).'

This suggests that the *qi* (氣) can be summoned by the *yi* (意), which is understandable if we think of the *yi* as our inner behaviour, the functioning of the mind. The *qi* is guided by what is in the heart/mind. I cannot concentrate my *qi* and keep the *qi* in good order if my heart is not functioning well. The heart sends the *qi*, and the spirits also send the *qi*. But if the heart sends the *qi* according to the momentary reality of my heart, that reality is formed by my *yi* and *zhi*. Both *yi* and *zhi* have the ability to guide the *qi*, because my mind is not different from the content of my mind. What is the difference between an anger arising within, or being angry, or becoming an angry person?

Chunqiu Fanlu (2nd C BCE)

'When the heart/mind (*xin* 心) moves towards something, that is intention (*yi* 意). The most important thing in nourishing life (*yang sheng* 養生) is to take care of the *qi*. The *qi* follows the spirits in order to become perfect and complete. The spirits follow the *yi* to manifest themselves. When the *yi* is tired and exhausted and when the spirits are agitated, then the *qi* are diminished, and when the *qi* are diminished it is difficult to have a long life.'

Here we can see the relationship with the *qi*. The *qi* follow the spirits. In many of the modern books, in China as well as in the West, *shen* is translated as the mind – emotion and psychology. This is both right and wrong. It is right because the spirits are what the heart/mind is and how it functions. We cannot say that we have spirits within us that are not 'us'. If I have a spirit within me which is not 'me', then what is it? It must be some kind of possession. My spirits are what I am, and what I am is my heart, and my heart is all the ways that I feel, react, have emotions, desires, thoughts, etc. From this point of view it is quite possible to say that *shen* is the functioning of the heart/mind. But the heart has a model for its functioning. It has the ability to perceive the reality of its own nature, and to perceive the reality of things outside itself.

For instance, in the text of the Great Learning, we are told to investigate things, but how are we to do this? By our learning. But we also have within us the possibility to discover the natural order of life, which is heaven. In the human heart/mind there is not only the function, and what enables function, but a possibility to have access to the natural movement of life. Within, this is to return to my true nature, and without, to discover the natural organization of life (*li* 理). The ability to discover the natural order of life is the same thing as spirit, and it is part of human destiny to become more and more spirit-like – which means not simply that the heart functions well, but that the heart functions more and more closely to the spirit of heaven. The heart can know with discernment. So the spirits are also more than the mind.

In the Chunqiu Fanlu, the spirits follow the *yi* in order to manifest themselves. The spirits here are the functioning of the heart/mind. They cannot manifest themselves unless it is through the functioning of the heart/mind, and here it is through the *yi*. The *yi* gives guidance to the heart and to the *qi*. We see this in *tai ji* or *qi gong*, or any kind of martial art. In the context of martial arts, the *yi* is often spoken of in terms of holding a particular image in the mind, not simply executing a move. It is not enough to make the movement, even if the movement is perfect – it is not enough to know that you are imitating the movement of the tiger, you have to nourish the heart with images befitting the tiger and this quality of *qi*. If I am doing the movement of the tiger, I have to think of the majestic quality of the tiger in the wild forest. This is the way that the *qi* is guided. If I have another thought in my heart, then I am giving a contradictory signal to the *qi*.

Qi is a reality, not an abstract concept. And if it is a reality, then it is not simply a matter of the movement of the body, it is what is in my heart when I do the movement that is important – for the heart/mind is guiding the *qi* and enabling the correct movement. Chinese thinking is always practical. There is no point in just understanding mentally, it is about doing and being.

Guanzi Neiye:

'The way (*dao* 道) is what gives form to the heart/mind (*xin* 心). But human beings cannot hold it in place. Going, it may not return; coming, it may not stay. How still! No-one hears its sound (*yin* 音,

note, resonance). How immediate! Residing within our minds.'

This is a description of what is within the heart. There is no form, no sound, nothing; but there is a possibility of discernment in the functioning of the heart and the *yi*.

'That way's inner reality (*qing* 情) rejects sound and speech. Only after cultivating one's mind and quieting one's power of awareness (*yi* 意) may the way be comprehended.'

We cultivate the heart and the *yi* in quietness. But here, in a text written at the end of the 4th century BCE, there is already a link between the functioning of the mind, the rectification of the heart and the cultivation of the *yi*.

'When our heart is well regulated (*zhi* 治), our sense organs are well regulated (*zhi* 治) too. When our minds are at ease, our sense organs are at ease too. What regulates (*zhi* 治) them is the heart. What sets them at ease is the heart. Therefore the heart contains an inner heart. That is to say that within the heart there is another heart. …In the heart of the heart, the power of awareness (*yi* 意) comes before sound.'

So within the physical heart, which pumps the blood, there is another heart which is the functioning of the mind, the ability to react, have emotions, etc. But within this heart there is another heart which is the ability to connect with our own true nature, and the true nature of things.

As it is said in the commentary to the Book of Rites, the human heart is the heart of the universe. It is the same vision here, and it is also the same in medicine. The spirits manifest themselves through the functioning of the heart, permeating the body through the blood. So the heart within the heart is before sound; and before sounds, before words or elaborate thinking, there is *yi*. It is before the conception of an idea or a perception. The power of awareness comes before sound.

'After awareness (*yi* 意), comes form (*xing* 形).'

Because we have this awareness, everything can take a form in the mind, which is one of the reasons for the link in medicine with the spleen and the earth element.

'After forms, come words. After words, comes putting the mind to use. Without proper regulation (*zhi* 治) there will certainly be confusion. If there is confusion, there is certain to be death.

'Within there will be no delusions (huo *yi* 惑 意), without there will be no calamities. His mind complete within, his form complete without; encountering neither heaven-sent calamities nor man-made harm. Such a person we call a sage.'

Huo yi (惑 意) is delusion – *yi* which has lost its way.

'The forms of the heart/mind and the *qi* are brighter than the sun and moon, more discerning than father or mother. Rewards are not enough to encourage goodness. Punishments are not enough to discipline evil. But when awareness of the *qi* (*qi yi* 氣 意) is attained, the whole world will submit. When awareness of the heart (*xin yi* 心 意) is firmly rooted, the whole world will obey.'

Everything which is manifested within a form, including a mental form such as an image, a desire, an idea or a feeling, is rooted in the *yi*. Through the *yi*, the *qi* can be well ordered and well regulated. We can see in other texts that if the *yi* and the *qi* are not in harmony, this may put life in danger.

'The four parts of the body will be rectified (*zheng* 正), the blood and *qi* will be quiet. Focus the power of awareness (*yi* 意) and concentrate the heart/mind, the ears and eyes will not be distracted, and even though things may be distant they will appear as if near at hand.

'Being relaxed and humane (*ren* 仁) you will find happiness within yourself. This is called setting the *qi* in motion (*yun qi* 運氣), so that your awareness (*yi* 意) and action (*xing* 行) become like heaven.'

If I can make my *yi* like heaven, or the natural order, my heart/mind and my spirits will become like the spirits of heaven. So maybe we can begin to see why the *yi* is called one of the five spirits in medicine.

ZHI IN CLASSICAL TEXTS

The character zhi 志

In the character for *zhi* (志), the lower part is the heart/mind (心), and above, a character that is classically explained as a small shoot (士). This represents something that can form a base from which it is possible to grow and develop in the right way. Originally it might have been a symbol of the phallus, and it suggests a kind of directional tension of the vital forces. Zhi (志) fixes something in the mind. The *yi* (意) gives form to an image, a thought, a desire; the *zhi* then fixes that in the mind. It is almost inseparable from the *yi*, because, as is said in Lingshu chapter 8:

'When intention (*yi* 意) remains, then it is called will (*zhi* 志)'.

The difference between the *yi* and the *zhi* is a kind of continuity, there is no real difference in their nature.

This is very different from the couple of *hun* (魂) and *po* (魄), which are a *yin yang*, heaven and earth couple. It is not possible to say that about *yi* and *zhi*, because their nature has more of a continuity, they are similar concepts. With *yi* there is the beginning of intention, and will cannot exist unless there is intention. They have a complementary relationship, but they do not function as a *yin yang* couple. Together they make up the reality of the heart/mind; they build the heart/mind throughout life.

Zhi is to aspire to, to hold an intention, and to fix one's mind on it. It is to have a purpose or an ambition – a desire that is fixed in the mind. It is also determination, propensity or inclination. The quality of the *zhi* is not only measured by its strength, but in the direction in which it orientates the life, thoughts and desires.

In the classical texts we find that the only way to orientate the heart/mind is towards ultimate reality, absolute perfection or goodness. In a Confucian text, there is nothing higher than setting one's mind on perfection. This might be the excellence of conduct, which may be referred to as the Way. It may be the highest virtue, the foundation of all virtue, which is the highest sense of what it is to be human – and this is called humaneness, benevolence (*ren* 仁).

Lunyu (Analects of Confucius)

'The master said: Those scholar apprentices (*shi* 士) who, having set their purpose (*zhi* 志) on walking the Way (*dao* 道) are ashamed of rude clothing and coarse food, are not worth engaging in discussion.' (IV 9)

If you say that you have set your will on something – it must be something that you are willing to live and put in practice, not just talk about, otherwise it is of no value.

'The master said: Set your sights (*zhi* 志) on the way, sustain yourself with excellence (virtue, *de* 德) lean upon humanity (*ren* 仁) and sojourn in the arts.' (VII 6)

The will must be fixed on something – and preferably on an absolute, on something that is not limited but which offers a foundation and a meaning to humanity, such as the *dao*. If you fix your will on something that is not appropriate to the movement of life, then it is desire. There is little difference between will and desire, especially in medicine. If I want chocolate cake, it may be bad for my liver, it may be bad for my life, but if I fix my mind on that, it will not be enough to fulfil human destiny. It may not be a chocolate brownie, it may be becoming dean of a university. But it is the same thing. Are you the model of fulfilment of human destiny? This is the serious problem of the will.

If for instance my ambition, which is one interpretation of *zhi*, is to become the prime minister, I will do everything in my power to achieve that. It will take form in my mind and dominate my thinking. What I choose to do or not to do – all the desires that I have will depend on the establishment of my will, which is to become the prime minister. If I want to succeed in an exam, all I do is think about this success – I don't even think about chocolate cake!

So what kind of will is at the very base of my life? The texts say that our will must follow the direction of life. The only kind of will through which I can fulfil my destiny, is to set my sights on the *dao*, or what may be called the supreme virtue. If I set my mind on anything else, all the other wishes, desires and behaviours will be orientated by the function of this primal will. If I fix my mind on something which is not the movement – or the source and the end – of the movement of life, my wishes and desires and behaviour will lead me away from the movement of life.

For a Confucian, the first thing to be done in life is to set the mind on something. Something which is possible. Perhaps at fifteen I don't yet know the full meaning of being a human being. I don't know my destiny yet. So how can I discover my purpose? Perhaps by studying, by learning, nourishing my *yi*. So I have to set my mind on that.

> 'The master said: At fifteen my heart/mind was set (*zhi* 志) upon learning; at thirty I took my stance; from forty I was no longer doubtful; at fifty I realized the propensities of my natural destiny (*tian ming* 天命, heavenly mandate); from sixty my ear was attuned; at seventy I could give my heart/mind full rein without overstepping the boundaries.' (II 4)

Confucius set his mind on his destiny. He set his mind upon learning. Here *zhi* is determination. He was determined to keep to his direction. He had to cultivate his will.

In Daoism, it is important to become one with the *dao*, to integrate with the *dao*, by returning to the origin, the original *qi*. In this return to the origin, this integration of the Way, I will lose all desires and personal will. In the process of this return, I have no will, but at the very beginning (and the beginning may take forty years), I have to set my mind on that. We see that in a lot of Daoist texts of the 6th and 7th centuries CE. But the one who wants to practise Daoism, must set his mind on the Way. Not on the practice, but on the Way. And on everything that is needed in order to embody the Way. What is needed for this is a kind of courage. I cannot learn, I cannot practise, unless I have a strong will – a strong orientation which keeps me on course. It is very easy to stop. This is the force of the soul – the strength of the will – which is needed to keep this determination, and to remain in the *dao*. It is this kind of determined continuity which is suggested in the character *zhi*.

So the will suggests a kind of continuity. We no longer have will if we forget. In an extreme example, for someone who has lost their memory, it is very difficult to say that they still have will. To forget is a kind of disorientation of the will. So within the idea of *zhi*, there is continuity, memory. The character *zhi* (志) is also used quite widely with the meaning of a memoir. Something that is written in order to be retained and recorded.

If the only will we have is for the full realization of our own true nature, then this will can only come from the origin, where the true nature is found. This is reflected in medicine in the relationship of the will to the kidneys, which are close to the origin. A will which is not rooted in the original nature will generate all kinds of desires which will only serve to remove me from my true nature. Each time I fix my mind on something that is not part of the natural development of my life, I generate thoughts, desires, emotions and behaviour which are not part of the realization of my life, and are therefore damaging. Damaging my life is not simply a concept, because it will be damaging to the heart/mind and therefore to all the activity of my *qi*. There is the same connection with the *qi* as we found with the *yi*. If the *zhi* is what remains at the foundation of my life force, it is also my heart/mind. So the *zhi* also guides the *qi*. All emotions and desires alter the movement of *qi*, and all work on the *yi* and the *zhi* regulates the *qi*. The heart/mind is responsible for all the movement of *qi*. Gradually we come to see that *yi* and *zhi* are at the basis of what we call the heart/mind.

Mencius II A

'Meng Shushe's firm grasp on his *qi* is inferior to Zengzi's firm grasp of essentials. I wonder if you could tell me something about the imperturbable heart (*bu dong xin* 不動心), in your case and in the case of Gaozi?

'…The will (志) is commander of the *qi*, while the *qi* is that which fills the body. Where the will arrives, the *qi* halts. Hence it is said: take hold of your will and do not abuse your *qi*.'

What is in the heart/mind comes first; the movement of *qi* follows. We see this in the emotions, which cause the *qi* to change direction. It is because I am angry that the *qi* rises up. Of course, it is also possible that I become irritated because the *qi* are rising, but that is a different thing. Usually we see that what takes place in the heart/mind commands the movement of the *qi*. I am angry not only because something is irritating me, but because I allow anger to enter me. Anger can enter or not depending on the way I cultivate my heart. It depends on whether I can rectify my heart by taking care of the *yi*, the discernment of the heart, and the establishment of the will in my daily life. It is my reaction to things which changes the *qi*.

> '…the will, when concentrated, moves the *qi*. The *qi*, when concentrated, also moves the will. Stumbling and hurrying affect the *qi*, yet palpitations of the heart are produced.'

If my body acts in a way that changes the *qi*, by running and stumbling, there is also a change in the heart. But it is possible to regulate the body in such a way that I do not react with surprise and shock and I do not need to run and stumble. Then the heart will not be disturbed. The idea in this passage is that if we are able to regulate the heart, there will always be sufficient *qi*.

In the classical texts, the will represents all propensities and tendencies that may be found within the human heart.

Duke Zhao 25th Year

> 'The likes and dislikes of the people, being pleased or angry (*xi nu* 喜怒), sorrowful or joyful (*ai le* 愛樂), are generated from the six *qi* (*liu qi* 六氣). Therefore take care to model yourself on the appropriate categories in order to control the six inclinations (*liu zhi* 六志).'

Heaven has six *qi* (*yin, yang*, wind, rain, dark, light) which are sent to the earth, and the earth reacts by producing all life forms in an organization by five – five notes, five tastes, five colours, etc. This is not yet the full development of five element theory, but there is still an organization by five. This is brought about by the six *qi* from heaven, which together and in alternation, make the whole year with winter and summer, day and night, wind and rain. The response of the earth is shown in these groups of five. Human beings model themselves on heaven and earth, making use of the five elements for nourishing life. But when we speak of the six inclinations (*zhi* 志) they are patterned on the six *qi* of heaven. The heart is modelled on heaven rather than earth. And within the human heart there is *qi* which is able to produce life and which has to be guided and used with balance and harmony; if not we will lose our original nature. The six wills mentioned here are the emotions. And this is one possible way to speak of the emotions.

These desires and propensities are the ways in which I set my heart on something – either as a reaction, or as likes and dislikes, pleasure or anger, sorrow or joy. As a human being I have the ability to harmonize that. I need act in such a way that the six wills do not destroy my life, but help the *qi* to regulate and give power to my life. I can do that by imitating the pattern of heaven. Heaven never sends cold for the whole year. It regulates – and after a period of cold there is always a warming. Day and night do not have the same length, but they change and regulate themselves throughout the year. There is always a time of light and a time of darkness. And it is the same for the wind and the rain. They come and go. In the same way we must harmonize our will, our propensities, our emotions, everything that moves within the heart/mind, pushing us towards something or away from it.

Human beings should act in such a way that all emotions and desires follow the natural order. The natural order reflects the patterns of nature, so when we read in the text: 'take care to model yourself on the appropriate categories in order to control the six inclinations', it is suggesting to model oneself on the pattern of nature (heaven, *tian* 天), so that the heart/mind can discern with its spiritual brightness (*shen ming* 神 明).

So do we have one will or six wills? Or are the *zhi* simply all the emotions, propensities and desires that we have throughout our life? There is a relationship between the one and the many, which is always the case when we speak of something that is rooted in the oneness of the origin. I have only one will – which is the will proper to my life, and may be described as the will to live. But the will to live has to be rooted in my original nature. This is the will that I need to obtain, and I need to set my mind upon that. Of course, through that I have multiple wills. What should I study? What kind of career should I pursue? Who should I marry? There are a lot of things that are subject to my will – and at the same time are a function of the reasoning of the mind and my desire. This is the same as with the *yi* – it is still the realm of the heart/mind.

So will and intent also include knowledge, the reasoning and discernment of the mind, as well as the emotions, natural propensities, etc. All of that cannot be separated. *Zhi* is the will, the ambition, the fixation of the mind upon something, but it is also influenced by emotions and desires. If they are not part of my will, it is like living a lie, which was illustrated in the first text with Confucius and the scholar apprentices: they said that they had set their minds on the way, but they desired the opposite! It is necessary to cultivate the desires and emotions and to harmonize them in order to ascertain what is the most appropriate direction for my life, so that I may come closer to my true nature.

What is the will of a river? Or the will of a tree? The will of a river is to follow its own nature and descend. By following its own nature, and fulfilling its destiny, it will go to the sea. It reaches the sea by continuously descending, which is the nature of water. But how does a river reach the sea? By innumerable twists and turns. There are no rivers which flow straight. In China all the rivers flow east. But, the Yellow River may go north or south for several hundred kilometres. Is that wrong? No. It is simply an effect of external circumstances. Water never abandons its true nature, but it may go north or south if that is the most appropriate way to deal with the circumstances of life. It is not changing the direction of its will – it is simply adjusting to the circumstances of life.

In chapter 6 of the Zhuangzi it says:

'Speaking of the sage, they are sad in autumn, joyful in spring.'

Their elation and anger follow the change of the seasons. The 'fixed mind' is not a rigidity – it is to be fixed on the ultimate, but not on anything which is intermediary. The Daoist apprentice who fixes his mind on the practice of attaining the Way will go astray. He must set his mind on the Way. The one who is perfect does not have his own will. His own will is simply the direction of his life. Everything is done according to the circumstances, because he is free to respond to the circumstances of life. All his propensities and tendencies are simply what are convenient and appropriate to the situation. The river is always heading east, even when it is going north or south. It does not change its overall orientation, but it changes the route. It continues to descend, it does not lose its original nature. This is the meaning of the text of Duke Zhao 25th Year.

I like the example of the weather vane. It changes all the time, but what makes the change is the wind. But it changes with the wind because it has no personal will. If the weather vane wanted to indicate the north, then it would not be useful. It may always point to the north because there is something heavier in the north facing part of the structure. And once desire becomes so powerful that it dominates our will, our heart/mind, we cannot help but follow this desire.

The weather vane does not get blown away by the wind. It remains firm in its position, well rooted, and completely upright – just like the sage. As long as we remain in contact with our own true nature, these movements of the emotions and desires will not be damaging, they are just the normal activity of the mind. It is normal to encourage life and feel joyful during the spring, and to be just and severe during the autumn. That is the appropriate will for the season.

Lüshu Chunqiu chapter 4

> 'Those unable to teach, those whose will (*zhi* 志) and *qi* (氣) are not in harmony, whose preferences frequently change, who utterly lack a constant heart and who, as with clear or cloudy weather, become joyful or angry without reason.'

In this context, it is not because they are firm and yet follow the circumstances, that they change their mind, but because they are going with the wind. They do not have a root. They change their mind because they do not know what they want. There is no constancy in the heart. The only thing that can remain constant in the heart is the fulfilment of the natural order of life. And that is implemented by the form taken by the *yi* and the variation taken by the *zhi*.

YI IN MEDICAL TEXTS

In the classical medical texts the term *yi* (意) is used in different ways, many of which are an adaptation of the use we have seen in classical texts. *Yi* (意) is often used to express the meaning of something. For example, if the Yellow Emperor asks a question, he will often ask Qi Bo to explain the meaning of something, and the term used is *yi* (意). More specifically, *yi* is used for what is within the heart; the inner disposition of the heart/mind. I prefer to translate *yi* in this context as 'inner disposition', and *zhi* (志) as 'inner orientation'. In this context, *yi* implies a state of mind.

To assess the inner disposition of the patient is an important part of diagnosis. We see that in Suwen chapter 11:

> 'In all methods of puncture it is necessary to observe what is below, to follow the pulses (*mai* 脈), to examine the will and intent (*zhi yi* 志意) and the characteristics of the illness.'

So why is it important here to examine the will and intent, the inner orientation and inner disposition of the patient? It is the state of mind of the patient which will influence the outcome of the treatment, and the ability of the patient to work with the *qi*. As we have already seen, *zhi* and *yi* guide the *qi*, which is the function of the heart/mind. To examine the *zhi yi* is to look at what is in the heart/mind of the patient, and to examine the emotions. Suwen chapter 13 is similar:

> 'Link up with the patient; ask methodical and numerous questions on the patient's emotional state, (disposition, *qing* 情), so as to follow the intent (*yi* 意). To possess the spirits is radiant splendour. To lose the spirits is to be entirely lost.'

Here the *yi* is a much more general concept, it is not related specifically to the spleen. Will and intent are very often used in this general way to define the disposition of the mind, and are not then seen as two of the five spirits. The five spirits and their relationship to the five *zang* is very specific to the medical texts. But as we can see, even within the medical texts *zhi* and *yi* are often used in this more general sense. Here they refer to the inner disposition, which is dependent upon thoughts and emotions – whether there is anger or sadness, if the thoughts are going in one direction or another – all that has an effect on the movement of *qi*.

Suwen chapter 44

> 'If obsessive thoughts (*si xiang* 思 想) carry on indefinitely and one does not succeed in getting what one aspires to, then the intent (*yi* 意) is scattered uncontrollably outwards (*wai* 外).'

If one is prey to desire, and this passage refers specifically to sexual desire, then that which is at the root of the formation of desire is not simply something that I have created myself by learning, meditating, observing, etc., but there is some exterior object of desire. The building of what are the most internal structures of the mind, depends entirely on something external. For example, a man sees a pretty woman passing by and cannot help being drawn in that direction! It is stronger than his own reason. And of course it is the same thing with the chocolate cake! I am already out of myself – which is the meaning here. What is essentially my intent, the root of my thoughts and feelings, is out of my control. I am therefore 'out of myself'. This is a complete collapse of the *yi*, which leads to confusion within the internal organs and a lack of vitality.

The *yi* may also be said to be 'full' of a specific emotion, to be fully impregnated by the emotion. If I am full of anger, all that I say, all my actions and reactions are full of this deep incessant anger. And of course it is the same with the other emotions. We can see an example of that in Suwen chapter 22:

'In a case of emptiness (of the kidneys) there is pain in the chest, the abdomen and lower abdomen. The feet are cold, due to reversal (*qing jue* 清 厥) and the intent has no joy (*yi bu le* 意 不 樂).'

The text says 'that the intent has no joy', in other places we may see that the intent is full of sadness or full of forgetfulness – which indicates a very basic disposition of the mind. The lack of joy pervades the entire function of the mind. The intent is not related to the spleen or the kidneys here, it is just related to the heart/mind. And in this text the symptoms involve the relationship between the kidneys and the heart.

We often find this lack of joy, or being full of fear, or sometimes the inability to remember, associated with the *yi*. More generally the intent may be said to be calm or quiet, which is good, or agitated and disturbed. If the practitioner is attempting to examine the inner disposition of the patient, they can only do that if their own *yi* is calm. This is found in several texts, for example Lingshu chapter 9:

'Stay in a quiet and peaceful place; observe the signs of the coming and going of the spirits. Close windows and doors so that the *hun* and *po* do not dissipate. Concentrate your mind (*zhuan yi* 專 意) and unify your spirit (*yi shen* 一 神) so that essences and *qi* (*jing qi* 精 氣) distribute themselves as they should.'

Here I have translated *zhuan yi* (專 意) as to concentrate the mind. The heart/mind (*xin* 心) has to work on something. The capacity to think is one thing, but there is also the material being considered and the way to consider it. What is in the heart is the 'flesh' of the thinking, but the nature of the material also influences the way that I think. I think and feel at the same time. All that is within the functioning of the mind. The *yi* is much larger than thought. And here it means to concentrate all your mental ability and to unify your spirits.

The *yi* of the practitioner must be quiet in order to grasp the true meaning of what is shown within the patient. This is an example of the way in which the *yi* allows the functioning of the mind. If the *yi* is full of anxiety or agitation, it is not possible to understand the situation. We understand only according to what and how we are.

Suwen chapter 25

'With an intent which is calm, decide what is appropriate to be done.'

This is advice given to the practitioner. With a *yi* which is calm and still, it is possible to consider what the appropriate action is. And this is not simply a matter of calming down when you enter the treatment room, but a slow cultivation of inner calm that is acquired throughout a lifetime. It is not merely a question of stopping agitation, but of attaining a real quietness within. And real quietness is obtained when we are close to our true nature. If we are not close to our true nature, we cannot be quiet. There is always some kind of agitation and disturbance. With a quiet mind, we can consider not only what needs to be done, but we are able to observe and to follow all the change and transformation in the situation. We are not held to one idea. We can follow the change.

Suwen chapter 54

> 'Through the *qi*, human beings are correlated with heaven.
> Through the blood and *qi* to *yin yang* of the earth...
> Through the *yi* (意) of the heart, they resonate with the eight winds.'

This suggests that all the thoughts, emotions and passions of the heart/mind are changing like the winds of the atmosphere. The *yi* is like the wind, and we can also see that with the *zhi*. We must harmonize the emotions, and all that passes through the heart – not changing without also being consistent and rooted. Change is only made because it is the best way to continue in the movement of life. That is not a lack of consistency. So there are two things here. There are some people whose *yi* is constantly changing, and they are all over the place. But there are also others whose *yi* and *zhi* are changing, but only in order to adapt to circumstances. In order to be able to adapt, one needs a deeper and deeper rooting in one's true nature.

It is said in several texts, that when a practitioner has a good *yi*, which is nourished with a good knowledge and understanding of life – meditation, calming the passions, etc, this enables true discernment. We need a calm *yi* in order to have discernment, but we also need discernment in order to nourish the *yi*. This kind of cyclical pattern is part of human consciousness. This is what is called the activity of the spirit. There is always the aspect of the spirits which I may call 'my spirit', but also that other aspect of the spirits which is my constant inspiration and what I aspire to.

The idea of *yi* certainly contains the ability to focus the mind and to keep something in the mind, as we saw in Lingshu chapter 9. *Yi* is not only intention, but attention. It is to be present with the mind. As a practitioner, it is not only a matter of being fully present and focusing the mind on the patient, because to focus is not only to concentrate, but also to be receptive. It is having a true understanding, without changing or altering what is being received by any kind of personal feelings or emotions. This is the opening of the *yi* – which is being fully present to the other. It is also the ability to know what I want to keep in my heart, for example, a decision I made when I was fifteen to study. So it is to be present with the patient, with the other, but also to be present with the self, and to recall.

Lingshu chapter 8

This is seen in Lingshu chapter 8, where the presentation of the *yi* comes after the presentation in the text of the essences and spirits, *hun* and *po* – which all are the preparation for the appearance of the heart. Once the vital spirits and the *hun* and *po* are in place, the human heart can exist. And the human heart takes responsibility for the human being:

'That which takes charge of the being is the heart.
When the heart applies itself (*yi* 憶), we speak of intent (*yi* 意).'

The character we translate as 'to apply oneself' is interesting, because it is formed with the character for *yi* (意), plus the heart radical on the left (忄). This character may be translated as to apply oneself, to recall, to bring something to mind. To remember or reflect upon. Something is present in the heart, which is able to mould the heart/mind. But we are able to choose what we want to keep in the heart/mind, through its own ability to discern, through the clarity of spiritual illumination (*shen ming* 神 明) or through passion, desire, obsession, ambition, etc. The heart functions by accepting the light of the spirits and allowing the presence of what moulds the behaviour.

'When intent (*yi* 意) becomes permanent we speak of will (*zhi* 志).'

The difference between *yi* (意) and *zhi* (志) here is small, but what is in the mind gives form to the mind and also gives form to the will and the direction taken in life.

The emptiness of the heart is the ultimate *yi*. It does not mean that we have no intent, or inner disposition, but that there is nothing opposed to the natural flow of life, and nothing which occupies the heart by blocking it and so preventing the heart from being open to anything that is offered to it. There is no fear, anxiety, desire – only the joy of life, the deep calm contentment of those who are at one with their true nature. If the heart is empty, everything can be received. Nothing is seen as preferable to anything else. And here we see all the metaphors for the heart that we see everywhere, for example, as the mirror which reflects everything but does not keep any particular image. But of course the human heart always has its own identity, its own rooting and continuity. We cannot have any passions or desires, or even a personal will that becomes an attachment, because it is a distortion of our true nature.

Finally we can see the *yi* as one of the five spirits, and the spirit that is specifically linked with the spleen. This is also seen in Lingshu chapter 8. The first part of the chapter introduces the terms *shen, hun, po, yi* and *zhi*. In the second part, we see the link between each of these aspects of spirit and the five *zang*. For the spleen and the *yi*:

> 'When the spleen falls prey to oppression and sorrow, and cannot free itself, the intent (*yi* 意) is attacked. When the intent is attacked, one is disturbed until the disorder is total.
>
> '…the spleen treasures the reconstruction (nutrition, *ying* 營) the reconstruction is the dwelling place of the intent (*yi* 意).'

There is a similar idea in Suwen chapter 23:

> 'The spleen treasures the intent (*yi* 意), the kidneys treasure the will (*zhi* 志).'

It is easy to understand this connection, because basic functioning of the *yi* is close to the functioning of the spleen and the earth *qi*. I used the word to nourish several times. The *yi* nourishes the heart. To offer and apply something is specific to the earth *qi*. And specific to the action of the spleen towards the heart, for example in giving the best of the body fluids to make the blood and nourish the heart. If the heart does not have the correct quality of fluids, it will affect both the heart and the composition of the blood. If we do not have the correct quality of blood and *qi* nourishing the heart, there will be a problem in the functioning of the mind and the thinking. The movement of the earth is the same as that which we find in the spleen and which is also seen in the *yi* – the ability to take in, to receive and to mature. If I have a thought, I may keep and cherish it, or I may reject it, in which case the heart/mind must be nourished by something else. Otherwise I may reject something, but it may not go away! If I nourish my mind with different food – then it will be okay. I may want chocolate cake, but if I take some good nourishing lentil soup I will be satisfied. It may take some training, but it is possible!

When the *yi* is presented as one of the five aspects of spirit (*wu shen* 五 神) and represents the earth *qi*, the making of the mind, then we can understand the *yi* as representing the spleen. Once the correlation is established according to the five elements (five phases, *wu xing* 五 行), it is possible to take one of the correlations instead of the other, but in each case we are speaking about the movement of the *qi*. I may speak of the wind, or the *hun*, or the liver to refer to the wood *qi*; or the skin and body hair when speaking of the lung, as both refer to the metal *qi*. But of course it will not mean the skin as simply the skin, but the skin as a representation of the metal *qi*. So in the same way, the intent may represent the function of the spleen and the earth element, as we see in Lingshu chapter 8:

> 'When the intent is attacked, one is disturbed until the disorder is total. The four limbs can no longer rise…'

Here the disturbance of the intent is seen as a disturbance of the spleen in its ability to nourish the heart, and the ability of the earth *qi* to co-ordinate and harmonize all the five elements, so there will be total disorder. The spleen is unable to transform and transport nutrients to the four limbs, and so the four limbs are no longer sustained and nourished and can no longer move. So although it says that the intent is attacked, it is implied that the earth *qi* are attacked. It is not exactly the same kind of pathology of the intent that we have seen in other texts. This is the earth *qi* at the level of the mind.

Question: What about the *fu* here? There is no mention of the stomach.

No, because Lingshu 8 is dealing with the emotions, the mind and the spirits, and these affect the five *zang*. There may of course be an influence on the six *fu* or on the general function of the body, but they are not the rulers of the mind. The five *zang* are the rulers of the mind, and their unity is the heart. When we speak of the *fu*, we are speaking about another level. Of course, we see examples of craziness due to the *yang ming*, heat in the stomach, etc., but that happens because there is an influence on the heart. The stomach has no direct rulership over the mind, and even the gallbladder, which has a very special stature because it deals with the essences, is not mentioned in this text. In this case it is still the liver that has direct connection to the mind.

Question: I imagine that we might treat the heart in these cases, but if we are dealing with the *yi* aspect of the mind, would you tend to use points related to the earth element here?

The question is always whether we work on the spirits of the patient or not. No, we work on the *qi* of the patient. We cannot remodel the mind of the patient. That would be called brainwashing. But we work on the *qi* and it is through the *qi* that we are able to give signals which are received to a greater or lesser degree. These signals also come from who we are – our attitude, and the power which passes through the needle. But it is never a manipulation.

Question: But would you then consider the *qi* of the heart and heart master channels, or more the channels of the stomach and spleen?

The *qi* specific to the heart is simply the *qi* in its togetherness. The unity of the mind and the being is as we see in the Xunzi chapter 21:

'How does a human being understand the way? Through the mind (*xin* 心). And how can the mind understand it? Because it is unified and empty and still. The mind is constantly storing things and yet it is said to be empty. The mind is constantly marked by diversity, and yet it is said to be unified. The mind is constantly moving, and yet it is said to be still. Human beings are born with an ability to know, and be aware (*zhi* 知) and where there is this ability to know, and to know that I know [which is consciousness], there is will (*zhi* 志, memory). Will is what is stored in the mind and yet the mind is said to be empty because what has already been stored in it, does not hinder the reception of new impressions. Therefore it is said to be empty. Human beings are born with an ability to know, and when there is knowledge there is an awareness of difference. Where there is such understanding there is diversity. And yet the mind is said to be unified, because it does not allow the understanding of one fact to impinge upon that of another. Therefore it is said to be unified. When the mind is asleep it produces dreams. When it is unoccupied it wanders off in idle fancy. If allowed to do so it will produce all manner of plots and schemes. Hence the mind is constantly moving. And yet it is said to be still, because it does not allow dreams and fancies to disorder its understanding. Therefore it is said to be still.'

Xunzi is one of the greatest Confucian thinkers in the first half of the 3rd century BCE, and this kind of text was very familiar to those developing the theory of medicine. In the same chapter:

'The heart/mind is the ruler of the body and the master of its spirit-like intelligence (*shen ming* 神 明). It gives commands but is not subject to them. Of its own volition, it permits or prohibits, snatches or accepts, goes or stops. Thus the mouth can be forced to speak or be silent. The body can be forced to crouch or extend itself. But the mind cannot be made to change its opinion. What is considered right it will accept, what is considers wrong it will reject. Hence we may say that it is the nature of the mind that no prohibition may be placed upon its selections. Inevitably it will see things for itself. And although the objects perceived may be many and diverse, if its acuity is of the highest level, it cannot become divided within itself.'

This passage is also useful when we talk about the ego – or when we think about the nature of the self. The heart/mind is one – undivided.

So the answer to the question is to make a diagnosis – to see where the *qi* is out of balance, and the best way to regulate its movements. We do that through the usual tools such as the pulses, in order to observe blockage or weakness in the *qi* in a specific organ.

ZHI IN MEDICAL TEXTS

We have seen that the *zhi* (志) is also the functioning of the mind, and also has to be quiet – for example within the practitioner. We can see the definition given in Lingshu chapter 8:

'When the intent (*yi* 意) is permanent we speak of will (*zhi* 志). When the persevering will changes we speak of thought (*si* 思).'

Thought here is *si* (思) – which is not one of the five spirits, but one of the seven emotions, and which is also the result of the functioning of the mind. For example, if the mind is the ability to knit, and the *yi* and the *zhi* the two needles, the result is all thoughts, emotions and passions. A will which at the same time is persevering and changing may seem like a bit of a contradiction. But as we have seen – this is exactly how it is. There is a constant will which is the way I try to align my life with the natural movement. This is the direction of my life, the way I set my course. At the same time there are many instances of will which appear throughout my life. The variety of all of this creates the texture of my thoughts.

The will that is secure and constant has a relationship with the kidneys. It is easy to see the relationship, as in both cases there is a strong link with the origin. As you know, the kidneys and the water element are linked with the origin and beginnings of life. The water in traditional presentations, for example in the Hongfan, is the first of the five elements, and the number one is always associated with water. Within the body, the kidneys are in charge of the relationship to the origin. The origin which is One is manifested by the couple of *yin yang*, embodied in the two kidneys. The link with the origin is kept by the *yin* and *yang* of the kidneys, which are also the authentic or original *yin* and *yang*.

As we have seen, the will and orientation of my life must be rooted more and more in the authenticity of my origin. That is the movement of the kidneys and the water. Through the kidneys there is also the maintenance of the continuous flow of life – just as the river continually flows from its source. It is because the river flows from its source towards the sea, that the river has an identity. Its identity comes from the source. If it had another source it would be another river. Maintaining a continuous flow of life is also maintaining an identity. When we see the kidneys as responsible for authentic *yin* or authentic *yang*, one aspect of this is that all that is renewed within my organism, is renewed according to the pattern of my own life, in order to maintain my specific identity. All the *qi* which are continually renewed and acting within my body rely on this same source. The identity and the continuity are linked to the kidneys. In the will there is also a continuity of memory and identity. I am my will, because my will is my life direction.

Life is not an individual decision, but is made according to the mandate of heaven, according to nature. There is no real choice, but that does not imply that there is no freedom. That is a different concept. I have no choice but I am also completely free. This also has to be understood with this concept of the will.

We can see many possible associations between the will and the kidneys, and always with a similar kind of reference to the unity of the mind. The mind has to be one, but the will also has to be one. The will is the will of the kidneys, but it is also the will of the heart, and we cannot have two wills. There is simply a constant and consistent link through both the heart and the kidneys to the origin.

The will presented in the medical texts also represents all the desires, tendencies and propensities that we have, and is therefore a way to speak of the desires and emotions as the normal propensity of the *qi*, as well as their pathology. Suwen chapter 5 is the most important text for the establishment of the resonances of the five elements, which are presented in five parallel sections. Each 'element' has what is called an 'expression of will' (*zhi* 志) or an aspect of will, and in each case the appropriate emotion for each of the five elements follows; anger (*nu* 怒) for wood, elation (*xi* 喜) for fire, thought (*si* 思) for the earth, oppressive grief (*you* 憂) for metal, and fear (*kong* 恐) for water.

So why is the term 'will' used here? The will is the natural propensity of life. My will has to be natural to me, just as a river flows to the sea, or a tree grows upwards – that is simply its nature. So here there is an analysis of the will according to the five elements, and we see the same thing for the five *shen*. This chapter looks at each of the five qualities of *qi*, to identify their natural propensity: what is the natural propensity for the wood or the liver *qi*? It is to give an impulse and to push upwards. This is the movement of wood. And what does this kind of movement do within the will or the psychology of a human being? It gives the ability to move forward with strength and courage. And what happens when this tendency is not harmonized with the whole? When this *qi* is overwhelming, it produces what we call anger. When we speak of the five wills, it is simply the natural propensity of the *qi* of each of the five elements, but of course, if they are in harmony that's fine, but if one is in excess, there is a pathological emotion which is the sign of a disturbance. Then there is anger, elation, obsessive thought, oppressive grief and fear. We usually use the term obsessive thought when we are talking about *si* (思) as pathology.

So will (*zhi* 志) may be used in this way within the medical texts to define the emotions, but when the texts speak of the five wills (*wu zhi* 五 志), this is always at the level of the organization of the five *qi* and their harmony or lack of harmony. When we speak of the seven emotions (*qi qing* 七 情), then the stress is more on the pathology or disorder. Numerologically, seven is where the danger of disorder manifests itself. The potential of the disorder produced by emotions is expressed in the seven emotions. The five wills are a way to harmonize and regulate the five *qi*, which is exactly the same thing as to harmonize and regulate the six *qi* as we saw earlier.

The will is always at the root of the emotions, passions and desires. If we are able to maintain our will in the correct way, to cultivate ourselves, and to rectify the heart – the desires and passions diminish. The will is simply an expression of life. We see this is Suwen chapter 1:

'They restrained their will (*zhi* 志), and desire diminished. At peace in their heart, they felt no fear. They worked hard and were not exhausted. The *qi* followed a regular course. Each followed their own desire and all were content.'

That is because the will is not caught up by desire. On the contrary, the will which is nurturing the heart is the orientation of my desire.

Suwen chapter 2

Another aspect of the manifold will, and the idea of the changing of the will, is like the sage or true being, following the prevailing *qi* through the four seasons. This is seen in Suwen chapter 2, where for each of the four seasons, there is a presentation of the movement of the *qi* specific to the season and the result in nature. Then the chapter tells us the way in which human beings should model their behaviour on the natural pattern of the four seasons. We are told when to get up, when to go to bed, what kind of exercise to do to activate the *qi* of the season. And then there is a passage regarding changes in the will. In each season the mind and will must be adapted, we must position ourselves within the season. This is the same as with the practice of martial arts and *tai ji*, the will must be aligned with the *qi* of the season.

'In spring …one exerts the will for life, letting live, not killing; giving not taking away; rewarding, not punishing.'

'In summer …one exerts the will but without violence, assisting the brilliance of beauty and strength, which fulfil their promise. One must assist the flow of *qi* which likes to move towards the exterior.'

'In autumn …one exerts the will peacefully and calmly, to soften the repressive effects of autumn; harvesting the spirits and gathering in the *qi*; pacifying the autumn *qi*, without letting the will be scattered outside; clarifying and freshening the lung *qi*.'

'In winter …one exerts the will as if buried, as if hidden; taking care only of oneself, as if fixed in oneself, in possession of oneself.'

There is a variation or modulation of the will. The movement of the spring *qi* is to give life, to give birth and make things grow. Whether we are thinking of plants, lambs, spring flowers – the idea is that we do the same thing within ourselves. Externally, we respect life, and allow for the fertility of life, but we have to do more – there is an inner movement by which we are attuned to the will for life. In all circumstances, there is an inner determination to assist life.

In spring we help the development of life – as opposed to the autumn, when the feeling that prevails is to be strict and to limit by judging what is just and fair; not to let a crime go unpunished. In spring things are looser – there is more room for error. It is like the punishment of children for example. If they are young, we do not punish them in the same way as we might punish an adult. We try to encourage them in their growth and development, whereas punishment would be counter-productive. And this is an example of the way in which we can be with the *qi* of the moment. Of course, the four seasons are a very general pattern. And the *qi* of spring can also be seen in any other situation which is spring-like – which could be the beginnings of life. It is counter-productive to apply the rules for autumn to the spring, and to encourage in the heart of the child the will appropriate to the autumn.

The same thing may apply to all kinds of evolving situations which need a different kind of will at different stages. And of course all the cycles of life are mixed together to make a complex whole. But it is possible to become attuned to that, as different situations will present the same kind of *qi*. Again it is like the weather vane – we need to be attuned to the present situation, but for that we need the emptiness of the heart, which is able be present to the reality within and around us. Of course, this is all a part of good health. I cannot be in good health if I am unable to adapt to the situation, and this is not by chasing after something, but by being aligned to what is. If we practise this, it will become more and more spontaneous, natural and free. It is then no longer how I chose to be – it is simply how it is.

The will, which may represent all the emotions and desires, all the variations of the orientations of the mind, and which includes all the seasonal variation of will, is simply an expression of the basic will for life. I can only be attuned with each moment of time if I reside in my constant and correct will.

In several texts we see the *zhi* (志) as the mind itself. In some texts we translate *yi* (意) as the mind, and in others we translate *zhi* as the mind. All are possible, and all are also the heart (*xin* 心).

Suwen chapter 39

'When there is elation the *qi* are properly harmonized, and the will (*zhi* 志) spreads out well everywhere. Nutrition and defence (*ying wei* 營 衛) are in free communication and function well. This is how the *qi* are loosened.'

The blood is circulating well, so the *qi* and blood are harmonized, and the will spreads everywhere. The will is in the heart, and also in the *qi*, and in the whole body. If I want to move my finger, I am able to do that. The circulation of the will and the harmony of blood and *qi* enable that. The *qi* are harmonized because the will is harmonized. If the will is not balanced, there will be disturbance in the emotions, and also a disturbance in the *qi*. Here elation implies a feeling of ease within the body and mind, rather than excitement. The will is used in the same way in this text as we might use the mind, it is the mind acting with a purpose. We read in the Lunyu (Analects of Confucius) that it is not possible for a human being to live without a purpose. That is death. If there is no more purpose to a life, it is destroying itself. The cells will just disappear.

Question: So there is never any mention of five *yi*?

No. Definitely not. This idea of the closeness between the heart and the kidneys, the *shen* (神) and the *zhi* (志) is what is suggested here. And the importance, as we have discussed, of the relationship of the kidneys with the origin. Even in modern Chinese *shen zhi* (神 志) is an expression of the mind or consciousness. It is used to translate the western concept of the mind and consciousness. The will also has this relationship with the One. All the manifestations of the will are related to the base of the will and therefore reflect the heart/mind and the spirits. The *yi* is never one or multiple, it is everything that makes up and builds the mind. The *zhi* is the way in which that moves forward.

Suwen chapter 24 gives a presentation of good or bad health in terms of what may be called body and mind. The body-form is *xing* (形), and the mind is not the heart/mind (*xin* 心) but *zhi* (志). Here *zhi* represents the state and the functioning of the mind. When the body is in good shape but the will/mind is suffering from bitterness, then the disease is found in the vital circulation (*mai* 脈). If the physical aspect of life is tranquil and happy, there is no exhaustion from over-work, but the mind is overwhelmed by concerns and difficulties, obsessions, etc. In this case, the tiredness is not physical, the muscular strength is not damaged, but due to worries and concerns there is a kind of knot in the thoughts and there will be injury on the circulation of the *ying* (營) and the *wei* (衛), blood and *qi*. The pathology is seen in the vital circulation (*mai* 脈), and may be of emptiness from exhaustion, or of fullness if there is blockage.

In this chapter five different patterns are presented, and they are called 'the five variations in the relationship between the body (*xing* 形) and mind/will (*zhi* 志)'. Either you are physically fine, but your mind is obsessed by worries, or you are in a good physical shape, and you are quite happy, but there may be a tendency to indulge too much in various pleasures, like over-eating, which may cause blockage.

As we have seen for the *yi*, and its correlation with the earth and the spleen, the *zhi* may be used to describe the water or the kidney *qi*. There is a similar example in Lingshu chapter 8:

'When the kidneys are prey to uncontrollable anger, then the will (*zhi* 志) is injured. The will injured, one cannot remember what one has just said; the lumbar area and the spine cannot bend forward or backward, bend or straighten up.'

Here the injury is to the *qi* and essences of the kidneys. The inability to remember, or to hold on to things – an inability to listen and allow things to enter into the mind – is a deficiency of the essences of the kidneys. This is not the same kind of pathology of the will as we saw in Suwen chapter 24. This is a different aspect. In that case, the *zhi* represented all the functions of the mind; here, it is in relationship with the kidney *qi* within the mind and body, because the inability of the lumbar spine to move is a pathology of the *qi* and essences of the kidneys.

If the will has to be rooted somewhere, it is in the essences of the kidneys. The question is whether a diminution of the will may also lead to a diminution of the essences of the kidneys. The answer is that it depends on what has been achieved by the heart. Someone who has cultivated a good heart/mind, with a strong and well oriented will, and a calm balanced *yi* – even if they are sick and the kidneys become very weak, the will may be unshakable. There is a complete link between the mind and the *qi* and the body, but there is also a hierarchy. What is of the mind is not necessarily submitted to the body. I may accentuate that if I submit my mind to my body – but that is not normal human practice.

The will may also represent the functioning of the kidneys, just as the spirits may represent the functioning of the heart. For instance, Suwen chapter 62 speaks of an excess and deficiency of the will, but in fact the meaning is of an excess or deficiency of the function of the kidneys.

> 'In case of excess in the will, the symptoms are of swelling of the abdomen and diarrhoea with undigested food. Insufficiency of the will results in reversal (*jue* 厥) and symptoms of weakness of blood and *qi*, disorder in the five *zang*, and an inability to move the joints.'

That is not related to the mind, but we can see that in excess, there is an insufficiency of *yang*, an excess of cold, which results in dilation of the abdomen and diarrhoea with undigested food. In weakness there is *jue*, as weakening and reversal. This effects the whole body, but the weakness is in the kidneys.

YI AND ZHI AS A COUPLE

Very often in the medical texts we find *zhi* and *yi* together, sometimes this alludes to the spirits of the kidneys and spleen, but more often to the implementation of the heart, and the functioning of the mind.

In Suwen chapter 62 there is a presentation of the five *zang*, and each is related – not to the five spirits, or to the five parts of the body, but to a mixture of all that, which we often find in the texts:

> 'The heart treasures the *shen* (神), the lung treasures the *qi* (氣), the liver treasures the blood (*xue* 血), the spleen treasures the flesh (*rou* 肉), the kidneys treasure the will (*zhi* 志). All that makes a complete and prefect body. When will and intent (*zhi yi* 志 意) communicate intimately and join inside the bone and marrow, then the individual is perfectly completed with the body-form and the five *zang*.'

It is interesting here that even though *shen* is given for the heart and *zhi* for the kidneys within the presentation of the five *zang*, what is then referred to is not the *shen* (神), or the *shen ming* (神 明), or the *jing shen* (精 神), but *zhi yi* (志 意). Here it is the *zhi yi* that forms the reality of the individual mind, as it is the bone and marrow, which give the basis and foundation of the body-form. *Zhi yi* and bone and marrow represent the complete organization of the mind and body. In several texts the *zhi* and *yi* are said to be what rules, controls and governs (*zhi* 治) our inner life. We see this is Suwen chapter 3:

> 'When the *qi* of heaven are pure and quiet, then will and intent (*zhi yi* 志 意) govern (*zhi* 治) correctly. Following this good governance, the *yang qi* are firm and solid, and harmful influences cannot affect us.'

This image of the *qi* of heaven being calm and quiet, is possibly an image of the heart/mind; then the will and intent are able to govern life, and as a result of that all the *qi* will be guided in the correct way; there will be perfect defence, and perverse influences will have no effect. This is even more specific in Lingshu chapter 47, which begins with a description of the destiny of a human being, and how that may be implemented through the *mai* (脈 vital circulation), the *wei* (衛) and *ying* (營) and also through the heart/mind:

'Will and intent are what direct (*zhi* 治) the vital spirit (*jing shen* 精神), gather *hun* (魂) and *po* (魄), regulate hot and cold, harmoniously blend elation and anger…

'When will and intent (*zhi yi* 志意) are in harmony, the vital spirit (*jing shen* 精神) is concentrated and correct, *hun* and *po* (魂魄) are not dissipated, regret and anger (*hui nu* 悔怒) do not arise; the five *zang* do not receive perverse influences.'

It may be surprising that *zhi* and *yi* are directing the vital spirit, *jing shen* (精神), and the *hun* and *po*. But *zhi* and *yi* are in fact the implementation of all of this. They are the volition. What are the spirits if they are not the result of the heart. And the heart is the functioning of the *zhi yi*. The quality of the vital spirit and the quality of the *hun* and *po* souls depend on the quality and the acuity of the will and intent. The heart is not found in the character for the spirits, or the *hun* and *po*. But the heart is within the characters for will and intent. So the heart, through the *zhi* and *yi*, is the link to my actual and present life. At my death, *hun* and *po* may survive, although separately, but there will no longer be a heart, a will or an intent. They are the reality of my present life. They are the way that I am able – right now – to embody what is called the vital spirit. So it is possible to say that the *zhi yi*, my inner disposition and my inner orientation, guide the vital spirit and the *hun* and *po*.

INDEX

acupuncture points   110
ancestors   5, 8, 1, 16, 17, 26, 37, 59, 60, 66, 72, 73
ancestor worship   2, 4, 16, 62
anger   52, 140, 141, 145, 147, 148, 159, 160, 165, 168
anus   38, 54
autumn   42, 47, 144, 145, 162, 163

Ban Gu   29
benevolence   136
birds   99
Bladder 13 (*fei shu*)   57
Bladder 42 (*po hu*)   56
Bladder 47 (*hun men*)   56
blood   12, 42, 43, 48, 51, 107, 110, 111, 113, 114, 116, 134, 153, 167
blood and *qi*   23, 28, 46, 51, 57, 109, 110, 112-116, 135, 150, 164, 166
body fluids   46, 48
body hair   47
bones   5, 18, 19
bone and marrow   167
Book of Change   75
Book of Odes   124
Book of Rites   17, 26, 27, 33, 133
brain   49, 97, 119
brainwashing   155
breath   30, 43, 111
Buddhism   2, 31

Chunqiu Fanlu   130
Chunqiu Zuozhuan   18, 124
Confucius   27, 37, 71, 124, 127, 128, 137, 138, 143, 164
consciousness   3, 8, 87, 88, 112, 119, 156, 164

Daxue   126
dan tian (丹田)   33
death   4, 9, 16, 19, 44, 45, 164, 168
decision   112, 123
defence   115, 117, 163

dementia   45
desire   38, 41, 83, 99, 117, 119, 123, 124, 136, 139, 143, 152, 160, 161, 163
destiny   51, 80, 119, 131
diagnosis   113, 115
digestive tract   46
door of the *po*   24
dreams   10, 11, 12, 13, 37, 42, 56, 98, 156

ears   76, 115
earth   41, 159
Eastern Zhou   62
ecstatic journey   37
eight trigrams   78
eight winds   150
elation   52
emotion   15, 30, 76, 87, 88, 109, 123, 131, 143, 146, 157, 160, 163, 164
Emperor Shun   128
Emperor Yao   128
eyes   41, 49, 76, 97, 114, 115

fear   83, 152, 159, 160, 161
filial piety   17
fire   41, 159
five elements   57, 65, 103, 121, 154, 157, 160
five element cosmology   6
five musical notes   121, 141
five senses   76
five spirits   40, 42, 57, 65, 118, 121, 135, 147, 152, 154, 157, 160
five tastes   97, 103, 141
five *zang*   39, 46, 48, 49, 57, 65, 106, 110, 111, 113, 114, 121, 147, 166, 167
flesh   167
foetus   21, 76
four seasons   105, 107, 118, 124
fright   112
fu   154
Fuxi   77
funeral   23

gallbladder   155

gan ying (感應) 90
gate of the *po* 55
genitals 44
ghosts 2, 18, 20, 23, 24, 66, 102
ghost carriage 69
Great Learning 92, 131
Great One 14
Guanzi Neiye 130, 132
gui (鬼) 4, 19, 20, 24, 27, 54
gui men (鬼門) 54

heart/mind 12, 38, 39, 41, 48, 49, 76, 89, 90, 95, 97, 103, 106, 107, 113, 114, 115, 119, 121, 122-169
Hongfan 157
Huainanzi chapter 7 101, 113
Huainanzi chapter 9 13
Huainanzi chapter 21 10
human destiny 15

imagination 42
inborn nature (*tian qing* 天情) 80, 83, 86, 87, 92, 119
inner disposition 117, 118, 146 148, 152, 169

journey of the soul 5, 37
joy 141, 145, 148, 152

kidneys 12, 40, 111, 113, 115, 119 139, 148, 158, 159, 164, 166

Laozi chapter 42 79
licentiousness 81
ling (靈) 8, 16
Lingshu chapter 3 108, 110
Lingshu chapter 8 56, 107, 122, 136, 151, 154, 157, 165
Lingshu chapter 9 50, 148, 151
Lingshu chapter 10 35
Lingshu chapter 18 109
Lingshu chapter 30 118
Lingshu chapter 32 111
Lingshu chapter 43 11

Lingshu chapter 47   46, 51, 168
Lingshu chapter 52   46
Lingshu chapter 54   53, 106
Lingshu chapter 69   107
Lingshu chapter 71   105
Lingshu chapter 78   46
Lingshu chapter 80   115
liver   12, 29, 40, 43, 47, 56, 57, 137, 155
liver blood   56
lung   6, 40, 42, 43, 45, 47, 53, 54, 56, 57, 154
Lüshi Chunqiu   99, 145

madness   37, 44, 45
martial art   132, 161
Mawangdui funeral banner   28, 36
Mencius   124, 140
meridians   51, 111, 115
metal   6, 40, 41, 42, 57, 159
musculature   44, 47

nails   47
Nanjing difficulty 8   111
natural disposition (tian xing 天情)   76
natural order   5, 36, 68, 71, 74, 76, 86, 101, 108, 111, 116, 125, 132, 142, 145
natural organization, inner patterning (*li* 理)   77, 88, 131
needle   45, 50, 109, 112, 113, 115, 117, 155
Neiye   86, 94, , 112, 130, 132
no form (*wu xing* 無形)   37, 83
nose   41
Nugua   77
nutrition   115, 117, 163

obsessive thought   147, 160
oedema   55
oppression   153, 159, 160
oracular inscriptions   4, 60
original nature   143

palpation   112, 115
phoenix   60, 61
po han (魄汗)   55
po men (魄門)   54
pores   54, 110
practitioner   51, 60, 109, 115, 148-151, 157
pregnancy and gestation   20, 33, 76
pulse   146

qi gong   132

renaissance   3
ritual   4, 19, 23, 26,

sacrifice   28, 70, 71
sadness   147
san cai (三才)   74
sentient souls   38
seven *po*   22, 28, 31
shamanism   1, 25, 26, 70
Shangdi   60
sheng ren (聖人)   104
Shuowen Jiezi   6, 8, 61
six *fu*   46, 49, 111
skin   45, 47, 55, 154
Songs of Chu   7, 26,
souls of the dead   5
sounds   121
sour taste   47
spleen   40, 97, 122, 152, 154, 155, 167
spring   47, 144, 145, 161
Spring and Autumn Annals of LüBuwei   7
State of Chu   7
stomach   155
straw dogs   23
summer   161
Summons of the Soul   26
Supreme Deity   60
Suwen chapter 1   104, 160

Suwen chapter 2   108, 161
Suwen chapter 3   55, 167
Suwen chapter 5   103
Suwen chapter 7   55
Suwen chapter 9   47
Suwen chapter 10   56
Suwen chapter 13   106, 146
Suwen chapter 17   13, 114
Suwen chapter 22   148
Suwen chapter 23   46, 153
Suwen chapter 24   164, 166
Suwen chapter 25   149
Suwen chapter 26   110, 114
Suwen chapter 27   113
Suwen chapter 39   163
Suwen chapter 44   147
Suwen chapter 54   150
Suwen chapter 62   92, 113, 166
Suwen chapter 80   115
sweat   55

tai ji   132, 161
thinking, thought   122, 157, 159, 165
three *hun*   31
three powers   74
tiger   33, 132
tongue   41
trance   36
triple heater   111
true nature   149, 152

violent death   23, 31
vital circulation (*mai* 脈)   165

water   41, 158, 159, 165
wei (衛 defence)   49, 109
Western Zhou   62
white   5, 30
wind   103

winter 162
wisdom 90, 103, 114
wood 40, 41, 57, 103
worry 117
wu shen (五神) 65, 118, 154
wu xing (五行) 103, 154
Wuxing Taiyi 41

Xici chapter 2 95
Xunzi chapter 17 81
Xunzi chapter 21 99, 155

yang ming (陽明) 155
Yellow River 143
Yijing 78
Yili 25
ying (nutrition) 49, 109
Yu the Great 128
yuan shen (原神) 119

Zuozhuan 9
zhen ren (真人) 104
zhi ren (至人) 104
Zhuangzi chapter 5 96
Zhuangzi chapter 6 12, 144
Zhuangzi chapter 11 97
Zhuangzi chapter 12 79
Zhuangzi chapter 13 86
Zhuangzi chapter 19 84
Zhuangzi chapter 21 91
Zhuangzi chapter 22 9, 11, 100
Zhuangzi chapter 24 81

BIBLIOGRAPHY

The following is a list of texts referred to in the seminars, some English translations are included:

Baihutong, Discourses of the White Tiger Hall. English translation by Tjan Tjoe Som; The Comprehensive Discussions in the White Tiger Hall, a contribution to the History of Classical Studies in the Han Period, attributed to Ban Gu (32-92 CE); Sinica Leidensia, 1949

Chuci, The Song of Chu; English edition, *The Songs of the South,* an anthology of ancient Chinese poems by Qu yuan and other poets; David Hawkes, Penguin Books, 1985

Chunqiu Fanlu, the Luxuriant Dew of the Spring and Autumn Annals, attributed to Dong Zhongshu (179-104 BCE), but probably a collection texts of different authorship. A collection of mid-Han Confucian thought.

Chunqiu Zuozhuan, a commentary by Zuo on the Spring and Autumn Annals. English translation James Legge in The Chinese Classics; reprinted by Hong Kong University Press, 1960

Daxue, The Great Learning. English translation James Legge; The Chinese Classics Vol 1, Hong Kong University Press, 1960

Guanzi, Neiye; English Language editions: W. Allyn Rickett; Guanzi, a study and translation; Princeton University Press. *Original Dao: Inward Training* Harold Roth; Columbia University Press, New York, 1999

The Huainanzi, Major, Queen, Meyer and Roth; Columbia University Press, New York, 2010

Huai Nan Tzu: Philosophical Synthesis in Early Han Thought, Charles le Blanc; Hong Kong University Press, Hong Kong, 1985

Jing Shen: English translation of Huainanzi chapter 7, Monkey Press, London, 2010

La Banniere: pour une dame Chinoise allant en paradis (Mawangdui funeral banner), Claude Larre and Elisabeth Rochat de la Vallée; Desclée de Brouwer, Paris, 1995

Liji, The Book of Rites. English translation, Li Chi, Book of Rites; an encyclopedia of ancient ceremonial usages, religious creeds and social institutions. James Legge, New York University Books, 1967 (originally published 1885)

Lunyu, Analects of Confucius. English translation: Analects of Confucius, a philosophical translation; Roger Ames and Henry Rosemont; Ballantine Books, 1998

Lüshi Chunqiu: The Annals of Lü Buwei, Knoblock and Riegel; Stanford University Press, 2000

Mencius, English translation, D. C. Lau; Chinese University Press

Pregnancy and Gestation, Elisabeth Rochat de la Vallée; Monkey Press, London, 2007

Rooted in Spirit (Lingshu chapter 8), Claude Larre and Elisabeth Rochat de la Vallée; Station Hill Press, New York, 1995

Shuowen Jiezi: Explaining and Analyzing Characters; Xu Shen, 121 CE

Sima Qian, Shi Ji, Records of the Grand Historian; English translation, Burton Watson, Columbia University Press, revised edition 1993

The Complete Works of Chuang Tzu, Burton Watson; Columbia University Press, New York, 1968

The Heart in Lingshu chapter 8, Claude Larre and Elisabeth Rochat de la Vallée; Monkey Press, London 2000

The Way of Heaven, Suwen chapters 1 and 2, Claude Larre; Monkey Press, London, 1998

Xici also known as *Dazhuan,* The Great Commentary (to the Book of Changes) English translation, The Classic of Changes, Richard Lynn; Columbia University Press, 1994

Yuan Dao, Tracing the Dao to its Source: Huainanzi chapter 1, Ames and Lau; Ballantine Books, New York, 1998